P9-EES-955

Mutiny
on Koje Island

G. T. Hollewinske
Seoul, Korea
1965

Mutiny on Koje Island

By HAL VETTER

CHARLES E. TUTTLE COMPANY
RUTLAND, VERMONT & TOKYO, JAPAN

REPRESENTATIVES
Continental Europe: BOXERBOOKS, INC., Zurich
Australasia: PAUL FLESCH & CO., PTY. LTD., Melbourne

Published by the Charles E. Tuttle Company, Inc.
of Rutland, Vermont & Tokyo, Japan
with editorial offices at
Suido 1-chome, 2-6, Bunkyo-ku, Tokyo, Japan

First edition, 1965

Library of Congress Catalog Card No. 64-17161

[PRINTED IN JAPAN]

PETER BROGREN, THE VOYAGERS' PRESS, LTD., TOKYO

FOR GINNA

PREFACE

AT 3:15 PM on May 7, 1952, rioting Red prisoners of Compound 76 on Koje-do—an island off the southern coast of Korea which the United Nations Command had turned into a vast, sprawling stockade for Communist North Korean and Chinese war prisoners and civilian internees—seized and held as hostage Brigadier General Francis T. Dodd, commandant of the Koje Island installation, who had entered the compound for a parley with Red POW spokesmen. For the next three and a half nerve-wracking days, the camp commander's life hung in the balance while his Communist captors conducted negotiations with Brigadier General Charles F. Colson, his hastily appointed successor, for the fulfillment of outrageous demands which were scarcely less than breathtaking in their audacity.

UN Commander General Mark Clark called the episode "the biggest flap of the war."

Senator Styles Bridges, in a blistering statement to the press, denounced Dodd's "stupidity" and threatened an immediate Armed Forces Subcommittee investigation.

Secretary of the Army Frank Pace Jr. roundly condemned Colson for making "misleading and embarrassing" concessions to the POW's to secure Dodd's release.

Vice Admiral C. Turner Joy, senior UN delegate to the truce talks at Panmunjom, when informed of the Koje-do insurrection, ruefully predicted: "I'm certainly going to take a beating over this at the conference table."

It was readily apparent, even to the neutral Swiss representatives from the International Red Cross, that the Dodd kidnapping had all the features of a first-class United Nations SNAFU.

A fiasco it certainly proved to be for Generals Dodd and Colson. Before the month was out, both officers had been broken to the rank of colonel and packed off to temporary duty assignments in Japan, from which they were shortly afterwards returned to the United States to face the New Hampshire senator's investigating committee. Their Eighth Army superior, Brigadier General Paul F. Yount, was handed a rocket for failing to head off Colson's concessions to the Reds.

Twenty-twenty vision was not required—then or now—to perceive that the careers of Colson and Dodd were sacrificed to still the chorus of indignant howls in Washington for a convenient scapegoat.

But much more was involved in the Koje-do mutiny—General Clark's blunt characterization notwithstanding—than a mere military foul-up. Behind the events of Dodd's abduction is an amazing tale of Communist conspiracy and intrigue that would seem all but incredible were it not supported by an overwhelming mass of documentary evidence, including the matter-of-fact testimony of Pak Sang Hyong,[1] the North Korean Red political commissar who engineered the seizure of General Dodd from within Compound 76. Ostensibly a lowly private, Pak was in actuality the Red boss of the entire POW enclosure.

Not the least unnerving of Pak's admissions to UN intelligence interrogators was his revelation that the Koje Island riots were masterminded by none other than General Nam Il of the so-called North Korean People's Army, chief Communist delegate to the armistice discussions at Panmunjom. Dodd's kidnapping was part of an ingenious scheme to damage UN prestige in the eyes of the world, furnish grist for the Red propaganda mill by forcing the United Nations Command to create "martyrs" in their efforts to quell the intractable prisoners, weaken the UN bargaining position in the truce negotiations, and compel the UNC to divert badly needed combat troops from the fighting front to maintain order in the POW camps.

The most important aim of Nam Il's plan, however, was to exert pressure on the United Nations Command to alter its official stand on POW repatriation.

President Truman had already announced that no North Korean or Chinese captive would be returned to the Communist authorities against his will—a firm, humanitarian decision which the free world applauded. The Communists, on the other hand, stubbornly insisted every prisoner behind barbed wire in the United Nations POW stockades be handed over, at gun-point if necessary. Just as truce negotiations appeared to have reached an impasse over this issue, the deadlock was suddenly broken—much to the surprise of the UN team at Panmunjom—by a Red proposal to screen the POW's for purposes of determining the percentage of prisoners unwilling to accept repatriation.

The results of a preliminary screening offered a devastating indictment of the Communist regime. Less than 50% of the prisoners expressed any desire to be sent back to their Communist-dominated homeland. Many prisoners indicated that they would forcibly resist repatriation, despite a declaration of amnesty signed by top Red officials of North Korea and China. Communist prestige was at an all-time low.

In retaliation, the Reds instructed their agents in the UNC camps to foment riots among the prisoners which were given full play by Red propaganda agencies to demonstrate that the UNC was using coercion in an attempt to force POW's to refuse repatriation. They contrasted the horrible treatment that Red prisoners received at the hands of UN captors with their own "fair, humane treatment" of United Nations POW's.

Day after day, facing his opposite numbers across the conference table, Nam Il poured out crocodile tears for the fate of the Communist prisoners whom he alleged were suffering fiendish torments inflicted by the "sadistic and inhuman" United Nations jailers. Under a smoke screen of pious platitudes, Nam Il cooly directed the apparatus of subversion, terrorism, and political murder which throttled anti-Communist opposition among the POW's and turned the compounds at Koje-do into armed camps of Red defiance. Surely Nam Il's stellar performance in this dual role must stand as one of the towering achievements of Communist duplicity in the Korean War.

An intelligence summary prepared later at General Clark's UN Headquarters in Tokyo described the Koje-do affair as "a new area of total war." It was an area, unfortunately, with which our officers were totally unacquainted. Said General Clark: "...my experience had been with old-fashioned wars in which prisoners were people who had to be fed, housed, clothed and guarded, nothing more. Never had I experienced a situation in which prisoners remained combatants and carried out orders smuggled to them from the enemy high command." From the incidents at Koje-do can be drawn a lesson of fateful import for our future relations with the forces of Communism: the Reds have served notice on the nations of the free world that the Communist adversary remains a relentless, dedicated, implacable foe, even behind barbed wire. And he is apt to be most deadly when considered the least dangerous.

In retrospect it can be seen that the situation at Koje was produced by an amalgam of many elements: the huge bag of Red POW's that followed the smashing success of 1950 and 1951 military operations by the United Nations forces; the necessity imposed upon the UNC for a hasty evacuation of prisoners from their well-dispersed stockades when the intervention of the Chinese "volunteers"—MacArthur's "brand new war"—reversed the tide of victory; a weak, vacillating policy toward prisoners which ruled out the use of force in the first, rather than the last, resort as a means of maintaining order within the camps; a succession of POW camp commanders with little or no experience in running a stockade; the unwieldy size of the Koje-do compounds, some of which housed as many as 6,000 men within a single enclosure; the shortage of UN military personnel to serve as guards; the physical circumstances of the island; and even the ethnic character of the North Koreans who composed the bulk of the POW population in the camp. Long before Brigadier General Francis T. Dodd arrived at Koje-do to assume command of United Nations POW Camp 1, these ingredients had combined to produce an explosive mixture.

For reasons which are not difficult to discover, the American people have never been given a complete airing of the 1952 outbreak at Koje-do, nor of the months of accelerating violence which preceded the kidnapping of General Dodd. The Korean conflict, although it was one of the most thoroughly reported wars in our history, was a distasteful and, at times, painful subject to most Americans. Moreover, at the time of the Koje riots, the attention of the American public was riveted on the truce proceedings that were already long underway at Panmunjom. Whether or not there is any substance to charges that the UN Command and Eighth Army authorities deliberately soft-pedalled the Koje outbreak, it cannot be denied that newspaper accounts of these disturbances were shouldered aside by reports which described the quieter, but deadlier, cut-and-thrust taking place daily in the tents at Panmunjom.

Now, more than a decade later, it is time the people of the free world learned the full story of the mutiny at Koje-do.

CONTENTS

PREFACE *page* 7

PROLOGUE: *Operation Honeybucket* 15

CHAPTER ONE: *At the Inn of the Wooden Door* 25

CHAPTER TWO: *The Face of the Enemy* 45

CHAPTER THREE: *Morning Calm & Rising Storm* 59

CHAPTER FOUR: *...And Footfalls Lightly Planted* 79

CHAPTER FIVE: *Brainwashing—U.S. Style* 97

CHAPTER SIX: *A Study in Scarlet* 119

CHAPTER SEVEN: *One-Star Hostage* 123

CHAPTER EIGHT: *Generals Three* 135

CHAPTER NINE: *For Want of a Nail* 143

CHAPTER TEN: *Operation Breakup* 169

CHAPTER ELEVEN: *Sequel at Cheju-do & Pongam* 181

CHAPTER TWELVE: *Not with a Bang but a Whimper* 187

NOTES ON THE TEXT 213

APPENDIX I 215

APPENDIX II 217

ACKNOWLEDGMENTS 221

PROLOGUE

Operation Honeybucket

SMILING SAM was Koje-do's most picturesque character. Although his popularity may have been a matter for dispute, no one on the whole island—North Korean or Chinese, prisoner of war or civilian internee, ROK soldier or American guard—would have questioned his indispensability to United Nations POW Camp 1. His nickname, which apparently had been conferred by some GI with a sketchy sense of humor, was not exactly a perfect fit: Sam, an enterprising Korean businessman, habitually wore an impassive expression that a cigar-store wooden Indian might have envied. Which may have been merely an advertisement of his Korean antecedents; but more probably was a testimonial to the occupational hazards of Sam's homely profession.

Sam was what is called in rural America a "honeydipper."

He had a truck—a wheezing, asthmatic wreck—with the legend "Smiling Sam" gaudily emblazoned on its curving sides. (As one American recalled, "he didn't need a horn by day or lights by night. You just *knew* he was coming.") Into its cylindrical tank were dumped the malodorous contents of the sawed-in-half 55 gallon steel drums which served as privies for the POW's. According to a time-honored oriental custom, Sam's freight would eventually find its way to Korean rice-paddies and vegetable patches, where it would be used to enrich the soil as fertilizer.

Several thousand well-fed men can create a formidable problem in sanitation for a camp like Koje-do. Smiling Sam functioned as a one-man sewage disposal system with an assist from the prisoners. As regularly as a recurring call of nature, Sam's truck made the rounds of the camp for the daily "pickup." He was met near the entrance to each compound by a file of prisoners assigned—on a rotating basis, one hopes—to the "honeybucket" detail. The UN guards were quite accustomed to seeing these fragrant processions leave and re-enter the compounds. Consequently, as they passed a detail through the barbed wire, apart from giving the POW's and their "honeybuckets" a wide berth, they paid them little notice.

The Communist leaders of Compound 76 were fully aware of this state of affairs. As a matter of fact, the "honeybucket" brigade assumed a role of major significance in their audacious plan to kidnap the camp commandant.

Compound 76 was known to the UN personnel at Koje as a "tough" compound. The fanatical, hard-core Communists among the prisoners, led by Colonel Lee Hak Koo of the North Korean People's Army, had grasped control of the enclosure by the skillful and utterly ruthless employment of the same Red tactics which have been demonstrated elsewhere, on a national scale, with grimly unvarying results.

Beginning as a minority—a small, cohesive, ferociously disciplined cadre—Lee and the other Communist leaders first sought to fragment the opposition by creating mutual suspicion and animosity among their ranks. This was done by means of spies, stool pigeons, and informers who penetrated every prisoner group in the camp. Life in a POW stockade, under the best of circumstances, is apt to be lacking in opportunities for privacy. Secrets can only be kept with the consent of the majority. If factionalism is permitted—or, in the case of Compound 76, encouraged—to develop, distrust is easily converted into open hostility.

The Communists moved swiftly to capitalize on the dissension they had helped to bring about among their opponents. Against divided opposition, the granite solidarity of the Communist cadre proved irresistible. With outspoken contempt for the provisions of the Geneva Convention which specify the "free election" of POW spokesmen, the Reds installed their own leaders as compound bosses.

Having bullied and browbeaten the opposition into silence, they cemented their control by the calculated application of brutality. Discipline was enforced through the familiar apparatus of Red kangaroo courts—and sentences admitted of no appeal. Anyone suspected of harboring pro-UN sympathies—or any other kind of dangerous "deviationism"—was hauled up before one of these mock tribunals. "Trials" were generally held at night, after lights out. As Colonel William Robinette, a former commandant at Koje-do, informed journalist William L. White, if a man were found guilty "we would find him hanging in the latrine by a communications wire. In other cases, prisoners would be spread-eagled on the floor and stomped to death with GI boots—the crushed rib fragments going into the lungs to cause death by internal bleeding."

In another compound, the colonel reported, "we found five dead, but with no marks on the body, no water in the lungs. Then we found a small piece of cotton still remaining in the throat of one corpse, and knew all had been strangled."

The victims of these political murders were dumped near the compound gates, where the UN guards were sure to discover the mutilated corpses on the following morning.

"In yet another compound," said Colonel Robinette, "we found 14 who had been sick for some time, but not reported to the dispensary.

This was not a punishment: Communist vengeance is quick and ruthless. These 14 were simply to them otherwise useless human beings, whose death would reflect discredit on the Americans.

"Similarly, they were constantly harassing the International Red Cross with phoney reports against us. In interrogating them, they charged we drove slivers under their fingernails and that we used the 'water system'."

One imaginative genius, according to White's account, "insisted we had screwed his penis into an electric-light socket and, when he still refused to talk, had turned on the current, lighting him up like a 100-watt bulb."

Once the Communists had taken over a compound, they ran the enclosure like a self-contained Red fortress. They organized the POW's into military units, staged drills, exercises, and demonstrations, held classes in political indoctrination and Marxist theory at which attendance was compulsory, carried on a clandestine barter with the natives of Koje-do, maintained liaison with the Communist leaders of other compounds, flaunted the Red flag from the highest point in the compound, and—the final insulting touch—declared the compound off-limits to their captors!

And it must be recorded that the U.S. Army guards stayed out.

That a military commander could allow a situation to develop in which American troops were unable to enter a stockade holding prisoners of war who were in their custody sounds hardly credible. But to anyone familiar with the circumstances and the locale, such a situation is readily understandable.

Koje-do is a rugged island, with fist-sized rocks everywhere at hand as crude weapons. In addition, the fanatical Red POW's had armed themselves with a formidable array of homemade weapons. Colonel Robinette described some of the items in this arsenal: "In each GI shoe," he told William L. White, "there is an eight-inch sliver of steel. These had been sharpened into knives. Twenty lengths of barbed wire made a club, wired together and with a cloth handle. One of Koje's many stones, put in a sock, made a deadly blackjack. They made pikes out of Army tent poles, sharpening the pin at the end."

To have forced an entrance to Compound 76 would have been a hazardous undertaking by itself. And smashing the resistance of 6,000 recalcitrant prisoners, led by men who had already displayed their capacities for brutality and violence, would have required something very close to a full-scale military operation. It certainly could not have been achieved without bloodshed on both sides. This alternative, unfortunately, was wholly unacceptable to the United Nations authorities.

Affairs had reached this state when Brigadier General Francis T. Dodd USA came to Koje-do, toward the end of February, to take command of UN POW Camp 1.

He was the 12th commandant at Koje in the fifteen months that had elapsed since the opening of the camp.

By the time an officer in the U.S. Army attains the rank of brigadier general, he has amassed an impressive amount of detailed technical information about his profession. He may not, like Gilbert & Sullivan's peerless paladin, be encyclopedic in all "matters vegetable, animal and mineral," but he is assumed to be thoroughly conversant with the esoteric intricacies of supply, transport, equipment, training, weapons, strategy, tactics, etc.

General Dodd was a capable officer with a solid record of distinguished achievement. An Indiana-born West Point artillery officer, he had been serving as deputy chief of staff to General Van Fleet, commander of the Eighth U.S. Army, at the time he was ordered to Koje-do. If there was a blank space in his catalogue of military experience, it was one that had to do with running a POW stockade that numbered over 100,000 prisoners. General Dodd was a soldier—not a jailer. And he was confronted with a situation that might have taxed the knowledge and abilities of a Warden Lawes.

As a forthright military commander, General Dodd might still have proven capable of bringing order to Koje's seething compounds if the United Nations Command had seen fit to give him a free hand. But policy decisions over which he had no control barred him from the use of the only restoratives that might have yielded results. The bald truth of the matter is that the situation at Koje-do, by this time, had passed the point of no return.

Besides, even if General Dodd had considered the employment of military force on his own initiative and responsibility, the case of Colonel Maurice Fitzgerald, the officer whom he was replacing as commandant, would have occasioned a few second thoughts. On February 18th, Colonel Fitzgerald was called upon to deal with the most violent outburst from the Koje Reds that had taken place thus far.

The explosion occurred in Compound 62, another "tough" Communist enclosure. Before the revolt was quelled, 80 prisoners and one American were killed, and nearly 150 Reds injured. Nearly a full regiment of troops had been required to put down the riot.

By coincidence, Colonel Fitzgerald was absent from the island when the demonstration began. As soon as he returned, he immediately ordered a cease fire. But the responsibility for the loss of life was charged against him as CO. Shortly afterwards, he was given the sack.

Colonel Fitzgerald must have turned over his command to General Dodd with an audible sigh of relief. Nevertheless, Dodd can scarcely have failed to ponder the object lesson involved in Fitzgerald's removal. It was something to consider.

General Dodd decided to try diplomacy, instead.

A national news magazine described General Dodd as a "candid, friendly man who has admitted openly that he does not understand Communists." Officers considerably senior to Dodd have felt no compunctions about making similar admissions. As outstanding an officer as Vice Admiral C. Turner Joy, senior delegate from the United Nations Command to the armistice discussions at Panmunjom, had this to say about his countrymen:

> "Americans find it difficult to visualize a breed of men who fight Truth at every turn, not just occasionally, but always and repeatedly. Yet, the Communists are such a breed. Nothing is so perilous to their dark designs as the full, unveiled truth. I sometimes thought they would rather lie than tell the truth even when the truth would make a better case for them."

From his own background of experience, Admiral Joy has also testified that "the one negotiating factor that Communists respect above all else" is "naked, massive power and the willingness to use that power when necessary."

A power vacuum existed at Koje-do in the spring of 1952. And into that vacuum moved the Red bosses of Compound 76 with a plan for the abduction of General Dodd that was conceived in the mind of the man who stared at Admiral Joy across the conference table at Panmunjom every day: General Nam Il of the North Korean People's Army. Its success depended upon audacity, surprise, thorough preparation, unflinching determination—and a generous helping of American laxity and carelessness.

Unfortunately, all were present—or potentially present—at Koje-do in May of 1952.

The Communist leaders showed considerable imagination—a quality which is often denied them—in their preparations for the coup. Prisoners who were to handle the affair were carefully selected and drilled to perfection in their various duties. Moreover, the entire operation was rehearsed over and over again until all parts meshed smoothly with one another. As an added stroke of ingenuity, the Red bosses ordered their men to create a disturbance on May 6th as a pretext for requesting an audience with the camp commandant.

During the morning, on May 7th, General Dodd was notified by one of his staff that the spokesman from Compound 76 was seeking an interview with him. A man less courageous than Dodd—or one with keener judgment, perhaps—would have summoned the Red leaders to his office and conducted the meeting under the watchful scrutiny of an armed escort. But General Dodd, who had already acquired the nickname "Fearless Frank" among his subordinates, preferred to deal with the Reds on their own grounds. Later in the day, accompanied by his aide Lieutenant Colonel Wilbur B. Raven, Dodd climbed in his jeep and drove to Compound 76.

He reached the main gate at about two o'clock.

Waiting inside the barbed wire were the compound spokesman and leader. Dodd ordered the guards to open the gate and permit the two prisoners to step just outside the gate for the conference. The Reds launched into a drearily familiar chant about inadequate rations, the need for additional clothing and medical supplies, and complaints about the behavior of the UN guards. General Dodd listened patiently. There were additional demands which concerned matters that Dodd was in no position to handle, such as the acceptance of Russia as a "neutral" nation in the armistice proceedings and the involved business of forced repatriation.

As the interview proceeded, prisoners within the compound began to bunch up against the barbed wire inside the gate to tune in on the discussion.

After more than an hour of conversation with the Red leaders, it became apparent to General Dodd that the whole discussion was taking a pointless turn. Accordingly, he decided to break off the interview. The time was 1515 hours—a quarter past three.

At that precise moment, sharp on schedule, the "honeybucket" detail arrived at the gate of Compound 76.

Neither General Dodd nor Colonel Raven were armed. But even if they had been carrying weapons, they would have had no chance to draw them. Before either officer was aware of what was happening, they were rushed by the score of Red prisoners in the "honeybucket" squad. Raven had enough presence of mind to grab one of the gateposts and hang on for dear life until the U.S. guards rushed to his rescue. Even then the prisoners would not let go until one of them had been bayonetted in the face.

General Dodd was less fortunate. He was spirited away to a "command post" inside the compound where he was quickly searched and his personal possessions were confiscated. The hideaway was equipped with a straw mat, a built-in bunk, and even a vase of fresh flowers! The Reds showed at once that they had not only planned the coup carefully in advance, but were completely assured of its potential success. Within minutes after Dodd's abduction, they broke out large banners which read as follows: "We captured General Dodd. If our problems are resolved, his security is guaranteed. If there is brutal act or shooting, his life is in danger."

An ominous silence descended on the camp.

Colonel Raven—still shaken by his near capture—was filled with apprehension for his commander's plight. A few weeks earlier, Raven himself had been seized by the POW's who held him for three hours, made him listen to their complaints about the food they were receiving, then turned him loose.

The minutes ticked by while members of the Koje staff put in an urgent call to Eight Army Headquarters in Seoul. Their message was pointed and succinct:

Dodd was in the sack, the UN Command was in the soup, and somebody had better come up with a whole bunch of right answers.

Otherwise, General Dodd stood to forfeit his life...

CHAPTER ONE

At the Inn of the Wooden Door

IN TIMES LONG PAST, a small wayside hostel stood at a crossroads in the province of Kyong-gi, a few miles from the swirling waters of the Imjin River. For centuries Chinese emissaries, travelling to Seoul on horseback to levy tribute from the kings of Korea, stopped there overnight to rest and procure fresh mounts. It was a humble lodging house for foreign dignitaries of such lofty importance and large purpose; and following the exchange of a Chinese yoke for one of Japanese make, the place lapsed into an honorable obscurity that lasted for many years, until—in 1951—the tides of fortune once again brought influential foreign visitors. The name of this hostel literally translated, meant simply "Wooden Door Inn:" Koreans knew it as Panmunjom...

By the beginning of the Korean conflict, exploitation of prisoners of war had been raised almost to the status of an exact science in Soviet Russia and her satellites. Communist policy toward United Nations personnel captured in Korea was, as Colonel Kenneth Hansen of the U.S. Army noted, "to retain as many free world prisoners as was possible—for brainwashing, blackmail, and bargaining—and to get back every Communist prisoner. This would seem to call for carrying water on both shoulders, but that is standard operating procedure in the Communist system. The Communist propagandist has a different story for each audience, secure in the knowledge that exposure of his contradictions will rarely if ever have the widespread effect of his initial lies."

At the very outset of truce negotiations in Panmunjom, the POW issue was assigned the highest priority on the agenda of topics for discussion that the Communists submitted. The United Nations delegation recognized immediately that this matter was one which could deadlock any armistice discussions before they had scarcely begun. Accordingly, with the approval of UN Headquarters in Tokyo, Admiral C. Turner Joy—senior UN representative—entered a motion to have the prisoner exchange item placed at the bottom of the agenda.

For reasons of their own, the Reds were not prepared at this point to contest the proposal. Said Colonel Hansen:

"There was, first, the question of who had won the inconclusive war. The Communists had taken more than 60,000 prisoners of war; the UNC, more than 160,000. But 50,000 of the Communists' prisoners had been Koreans whom they had 'released at the front,' that is, press-ganged into slave-labor battalions and prisoner of war guard units. So the proportion of prisoners of war, to the uninitiated eye, seemed to be on the order of 15 to 1.

"Second, both sides were aware of the fact that a proportion of the prisoners of war in the hands of the United Nations Command did not wish to return to Communist control. How large a proportion neither side knew—the UNC because its intelligence said the proportion was greater than the Communists expected it to be and verification of that fact would not help to get an armistice, and the Communist side because its intelligence said the proportion was very low...

"Even a low percentage of prisoners not wanting to return to Communist control was unpalatable to the enemy, however, and it was probably due to the steps the Communists took to reduce that percentage, and the fact that those steps took time, that the UNC negotiators were successful in getting the question of the prisoners of war moved down on the agenda to the next-to-the-last item. By the time the truce talks reached it, the Communists were ready with their exploitation of the prisoners for psychological purposes."

The prisoner exchange debate finally began in December, 1951. Both sides took positions which seemed to rule out at once any possibilities of arbitration, and from which there appeared little hope of an early withdrawal. The Reds, on the one hand, were adamant in their refusal to even discuss anything short of full repatriation. Every Communist captive, they insisted, was to be turned over to the North Korean and Red Chinese authorities without delay once the armistice agreement had been reached.

A strict interpretation of the 1949 Geneva Convention—which the Communists quoted whenever it was convenient and flouted the rest of the time—gave some support to the Communist position. Article 7 specifies that "Prisoners of war may in no circumstances renounce in part or in entirety the rights secured to them by the present convention;" Article 118 stipulates that "Prisoners of war shall be released and repatriated without delay after the cessation of active hostilities..."

The Communists, said journalist Rutherford Poats, maintained that "the words had no other possible meaning than repatriation of every prisoner, regardless of his alleged personal desire to renounce his homeland. The United Nations delegation replied that this interpretation would 'convert a document designed to aid the individual into one completely negating his rights. You are saying that the prisoner of war has a right to be handed over to you, and since he has that right he has the obligation to go back, whether or not he wishes.

We cannot believe that the framers of the convention had any such purpose in mind.' "

The United Nations position, on the other hand, was stated with equal firmness. Like his poker-faced Oriental counterparts across the conference table, Admiral Joy was hedged about by orders issued from the home office. "The United Nations Command delegation," Admiral Joy declared, "received instructions from Washington to propose that prisoners be exchanged on the basis of 'voluntary repatriation,' that is, each prisoner was to express his desire to return to the side of his origin or to remain with the side that held him captive."[1] (This principle was later renamed "no forced repatriation," in an effort to break the log-jam—with results that will be recorded in their proper place.)

Back of this decision—reached by officials in Washington despite an anguished awareness of the probable consequences, and carried out with grave misgivings by the staff at Panmunjom—lies a grim story. The memory of certain bitter experiences in World War II, as *U.S. News & World Report* pointed out, was deeply inscribed in the minds of responsible American leaders, both civil and military:

> "At war's end, the Western Allies rounded up and forcibly returned to Communist Russia the Russian soldiers who had been captured by the German Army or who had escaped during the war. What happened then was one of the more gruesome episodes in the bloodiest war of history.
>
> "Thousands of Russians committed suicide rather than return home. Great numbers were herded into trains, trucks and ships, and forcibly transported to Russian-held territory. Of these, large numbers were executed on the spot by Russian MVD (secret police) officials. Others were moved to Moscow for mass trials and then executed. One Russian general, who had been captured, is reported

to have been decapitated, his head paraded through Moscow. Most of the remaining ex-prisoners were shipped off to labor camps in the least desirable parts of Siberia, where little has been heard from them since.

"To this day, Russian commanders use the experience of World War II prisoners to frighten Russian troops from having contact with the West. Desertions from Russian forces in Germany, once numerous, are now described as rare. The story brought by escapees from East Germany is that Soviet commanders still execute Russian soldiers before assembled troops with the explanation that the men executed had surrendered or deserted and then had been turned back to the Russians by Americans to be shot or hanged.

"For propaganda purposes, the United States thus has the reputation in Russia of a nation that will forcibly return for execution or for a life of slavery in Siberia any Russian who may seek to escape from Communism. The evidence is the standing example of what happened to hundreds of thousands of war prisoners who fell into American and British hands after the defeat of Germany.

"If now, in Korea, the U. S. uses force to drive its prisoners of war back into Communist hands, that reputation will be sealed—as American officials see it. They know that most Chinese and North Korean prisoners, if forced to go home against their will, will face execution, torture or slave labor as an example to discourage other Communists from becoming prisoners. The idea then would be strengthened that it is better to take a chance on death in battle than to fall into American hands and then be turned back to certain death or slavery at the hands of the Communist regime.

"In the event that Russia later should attack, nations of the West have reason to hope that whole Russian armies may want to surrender or go over to the non-Communist side. It could happen in another war, provided the troops involved were convinced that they would not later be sent back to face the firing squads of Communist rulers. The view of American officials is that Western nations cannot afford, in their own interest, to force war prisoners in Korea back into Communist hands against their will for that reason.

"The story of defections from Russian forces in World War II and the fate of those who did defect or become prisoners, thus, is behind the decision not to compromise on the last major issue of the Korean truce negotiations."

It cannot be denied that, humanitarian considerations notwithstanding, Washington's insistence on voluntary repatriation was strengthened by the desire to win a propaganda victory over the Communists which might supply a deterrent to future aggression. The refusal of any significant portion of UN-held captives to return to Red domination, it was felt, would constitute a major setback to Communist subversive activity.

Admiral Joy was frankly dubious. "An important fact to remember about these captured personnel," he warned, "is that they were *captured.* The overwhelming majority of these people did not come rushing into our arms voluntarily... Almost all had been taken prisoner at the point of United Nations Command guns. Prior to that time, they had been energetically killing, wounding, or firing at United Nations Command personnel. Only a minute number were 'surrendered personnel' who had come to our side because of hope for a better life. They were prisoners of war in the truest sense of the word."

In addition, Joy was cognizant of the potential dangers involved in this decision:

"First, the 'voluntary repatriation' principle would jeopardize recovery of all United Nations Command personnel. Second, it would extend the negotiations, thus extending the period of captivity for the prisoners, and extending the war with its attendant casualties. Third, the principle of voluntary repatriation was an arbitrary one, commanding no solid support in the Geneva Conventions... Fourth, to require prisoners to make a highly important and permanent choice under the conditions of imprisonment was to ask of them a decision they were probably not best prepared to make. Fifth, voluntary repatriation would establish a dangerous precedent which might well react to our disadvantage in future conflicts with Communist powers. Should they ever hold a preponderance of prisoners, we would have no recourse if they refused neutral visits to their prisoner camps and said that none of our men wished to be repatriated. Sixth, it was a political issue which strictly had no place in a military armistice agreement. A military armistice agreement should be no more than an agreement between opposing commanders to stop fighting. It should never be concerned with political questions."

Admiral Joy had a quite understandable reluctance to indorse a position which "placed the welfare of ex-Communist soldiers above that of our own United Nations Command personnel in Communist prison camps, and above that of our United Nations Command personnel still on the battle line in Korea. I wanted our men back as soon as we could get them. Since we were not allowed to achieve a victory, I wanted the war halted."

But abandonment or compromise were out of the question. "After holding in POW camps and listing as war prisoners Koreans who deserted to escape Communism," said Rutherford Poats; "after cloaking the principle of free choice for war prisoners in the language of historic significance, after picturing it as an essential precedent for any future war with a Communist enslaved people, we could not easily cast the principle aside to buy an earlier truce."

On this point, for the next three months, negotiations remained at a virtual standstill.

By March of 1952, a faint glimmer of compromise illuminated the otherwise somber landscape at Panmunjom. As a result of consultations with Washington, the UN delegates discarded the "voluntary repatriation" formula for one which specified, instead, "no forced repatriation." The change in wording was subtle, but significant, for it offered a face-saving loophole—if the Reds chose to wriggle through it. Nevertheless, we were obliged to point out that a goodly fraction of the 170,000 Communist POW's we presently held—a figure which included the 38,000 Koreans who had been reclassified as Civilian Internees—would undoubtedly resist repatriation.

Admiral Joy sat back and waited for the usual pyrotechnics display from the Communist contingent.

For once it was not forthcoming. Instead, the Reds were as gentle as one of their omnipresent Picasso peace doves. With dulcet reasonableness, they merely wanted to know how many prisoners would turn down repatriation.

Now the United Nations Command, as Colonel Hansen has stated, "Knew the proportion of prisoners of war who had freely surrendered in Korea, in distinction to being forcibly, physically captured, but that was an item of intelligence it was not, and still is not, about to give the Communists. However, it did not know what percentage of the surrenderees were so anti-Communist that they would renounce their homes and families, and what percentage had surrendered to escape, simply, the prospect of probable death. Nor did it know what proportion of captives, released from overt Communist domination in the prisoner of war camps and given decent treatment at UNC hands, might decide against repatriation."

We had to tell the Communists, therefore, that we could only guess.

"Now," said William L. White, "came a pivotal moment which no one in the tent then thought was of the slightest importance. On April 2, 1952, as they sat around the table, China's Colonel Tsai spoke up casually.

"Why, he asked, did we not screen them, so that they could know just how many non-returnees this would involve?

"We pointed out that this would take some time. Colonel Tsai, now the most reasonable of men, agreed. He went on to suggest that the Armistice negotiations might adjourn, until we complete the screening.

"Both of these sensible proposals were now adopted. But just before the meeting broke up, we came in with an after-thought. A good many of the prisoners we held seemed apprehensive about what might happen when they got back to their Communist homelands.

"So now, we continued, it might be helpful if they gave us an amnesty statement, which we could read to their men, promising a warm welcome on their return.

"They agreed to furnish this as easily as we had accepted their idea of a screening. April 2nd was a Red-letter day of Capitalist-Communist harmony at Panmunjom..."

April 1st would have been an even more appropriate day—all things considered. Secure in the knowledge that orders had gone out to the Red compound leaders to register their truculent charges as 100% in favor of repatriation, and to forcibly resist any efforts on the part of the UNC to screen the prisoners individually, Nam Il and his colleagues could afford to be amiable with the foolish Americans.

It is a scathing commentary on the suppressive features of Red totalitarianism and the callous cynicism of its leaders that the Communist negotiators received the suggestion regarding a declaration of amnesty without batting an eyelash.

From loudspeaker trucks and public address systems mounted on posts in the POW compounds, the text of the amnesty declaration—which had been initialled by General Nam Il of the North Korean Democratic People's Republic (sic), and General Peng Teh-Huai of the Chinese People's Volunteer Army (sic)—was broadcast to the prisoners on Koje for two straight days. It was preceded by the following announcement from the United Nations Command:

"All prisoners of war will be individually interviewed in the next few days. This interview is being conducted for the purpose of determining which prisoners of war desire to be repatriated to the Korean People's Army or to the Chinese People's Volunteers, and which ones have compelling reasons which they feel would make it impossible for them to return to their own side. This determination will speed up the rate of repatriation at the time prisoners of war are exchanged.

"At this time I must caution you that the decision you make is a most important one, possibly the most vital one you will ever be called upon to make. You must most carefully consider each aspect of the matter. You must make your own decision and for your own safety it is essential that you do not discuss this matter with others and above all that you let no other person, even your best friend, know what your decision will be prior to the time you are asked for it by the interviewer.

"To those prisoners of war who are not violently opposed to repatriation, the United Nations Command will guarantee return to your authorities at the time prisoners of war are exchanged. Your decision in this matter will be considered final. The UNC can make no guarantee whatever as to the ultimate fate of those who refuse to go back to their own people.

"Before any of you, for any reason which you think may be compelling, decides irrevocably to reject repatriation, you must consider the effect of your decision on your family. The fact that you are a POW has been reported to your authorities and they know that you are alive and well. If you fail to return, the Communists will undoubtedly consider your family suspect. You may well never see your family again. You must consider this matter from every angle.

"If your final decision is that you are violently opposed to repatriation, you may undoubtedly be held in custody here on Koje-do for many long months. However, the UNC cannot house and feed you forever. The United Nations Command can make no promises regarding your future. In particular, the UNC cannot and will not guarantee to send you to any certain place. This is a matter which you should consider most carefully.

"Interviews will be conducted in each compound to prepare rolls of the prisoners of war to be repatriated. Rosters by battalion have already been prepared.

"Within a few days interview points will be established near the sally port in each compound. At the appointed hour prisoners of war will be formed by battalion according to roster. Unarmed UNC clerks and U. S. MPs will enter the compound to conduct the interviews. Prisoners of war will move to the interview point when called by the clerks, where they will be asked to express their decisions. They will carry their equipment and clothing with them.

"Depending upon each individual's decision, he will remain in his present compound or be moved immediately.

"After individual interview, prisoners of war who are to be repatriated will be housed in compounds separate from those prisoners of war who strongly oppose repatriation.

"You are reminded that quiet and good order must be maintained within the compound during the conduct of these interviews."

The very wording of the above text—uncompromising to the point of grimness—makes it unmistakably clear that the United Nations Command was not about to practice any "hard sell" tactics with the Red POW's. No rosyhued, alluring portraits of life in the non-Communist world were going to be exhibited for the benefit of the prisoners. The UNC was determined to forestall any Red charges that the captives had been unfairly seduced from their true intentions by mercenary capitalist lures.

Chinese prisoners were quartered, at this time, in four compounds of unequal size. The largest of these contained over 8,000 POW's and was considered by the UNC camp personnel to be predominantly anti-Communist in sympathy. Next in size was an enclosure with approximately 6,000 men. This, too, was judged to be an anti-Communist compound—an educated guess.

Trouble was anticipated with the two smaller pro-Communist compounds. The UNC staff fully expected that the Red prisoners in these compounds would seek to bar the screening teams from admittance. Consequently, it came as a surprise when the Communist leaders consented to individual questioning of their men. One suspects that the reason for this sudden cordiality is bound up with matters of "face:" no amount of "proletarian brothers-in-arms" propaganda from Peking or Pyong yang was likely to persuade the Chinese "volunteers" to accept their Korean proteges as equals. And it is a safe bet that even the most seasoned Communist leaders among the Chinese could not stomach orders from Nam Il, whom they regarded as an inferior.

Screening operations got underway on the morning of April 8, 1952 —the "date of the first victory for the free world in the battle for voluntary repatriation," as Colonel Hansen described it—in the largest of the four Chinese compounds. In temporary booths, isolated to insure privacy, each of the more than 8,000 prisoners received a private and personal interview. Everything possible was done to prevent intimidation or coercion from either Communist or anti-Communist elements among the POW's.

Each man was asked a set of questions which had been carefully selected to elicit true and unbiased answers. The prisoner's final choice—to accept repatriation or remain in the custody of the United Nations Command— was noted on his identification papers. "Since this compound was reputed to be predominantly anti-Communist and against repatriation," said Colonel Hansen, "if the prisoner elected repatriation he was taken immediately to a waiting truck for relocation in another compound. If he did not wish repatriation, he was taken, via the walkway between the two barbed-wire fences skirting the enclosure, back to his original quarters."

The reason for this precautionary move is readily apparent. Allowing the prisoners to remain unsegregated would nullify the effects of the screening by exposing the men to further persuasion or intimidation from both sides to alter their choices.

The questions asked by the screening teams were as follows:

1. Will you voluntarily be repatriated to Communist China?
2. Will you forcibly resist repatriation?
3. Have you carefully considered the impact of such actions on your family?
4. Do you realize that you may remain here at Koje-do long after those electing repatriation have returned home?
5. Do you realize that the United Nations cannot promise that you will be sent to any certain place?
6. Are you still determined that you would violently resist repatriation?
7. What would you do if you are repatriated in spite of this decision?

It can be seen that the questions were weighted heavily in favor of repatriation. Prisoners were made aware that the UNC was not prepared to offer any guarantees regarding their future. Each man was cautioned to consider his family and the possibility—the probability even—that he might be kept behind barbed wire at Koje long after the others who had selected repatriation were returned to China.

One finds it difficult to imagine how a fairer test of the prisoner's intentions could be devised. Credence was given in many quarters to rumors that the UNC authorities were hoping—unofficially—for a majority decision in favor of repatriation.

"The questions," Colonel Hansen noted, "were asked one at a time, and a reply was insisted upon before proceeding to the next question. However, if at any time or at any stage of the interview the POW expressed a desire for repatriation, the questioning stopped and he went out to the waiting truck. But even if his answer to the second question might be that he would kill himself rather than return to Red China, that he would fight to the death rather than return, or that he would risk death to escape before he would return he was still asked the succeeding questions so that he would realize the implications of his choice of non-repatriation."

Question 5 was a critical item. Militant anti-Communist extremists had repeatedly petitioned the United Nations Command to be permitted to take up arms against their former Red bosses. Now they had begun circulating rumors that Chinese prisoners who rejected repatriation would be sent to join the "Gimo's" Nationalist forces on Formosa. More than a year earlier, MacArthur had inadvertently touched off a detonation in the press by intimating that Generalissimo Chiang Kai-shek's army would be sent to Korea to reinforce the United Nations battle line.

Such rumors, of course, were utterly without foundation. Commitments of this sort would have toppled the fragile structure of armistice negotiations that Admiral Joy and his associates had so painfully erected at Panmunjom. The very wording of the questions themselves clearly indicated that the UNC was unprepared to make promises about non-repatriation in *any* location. The choice that confronted each prisoner, therefore, was one of the utmost gravity.

Despite the anti-Communist character of the first large Chinese compound, it was expected that a certain percentage of the prisoners, perhaps as many as one-third, would accept repatriation for personal reasons—from an understandable desire to be reunited with their families. The only alternative which the United Nations Command was empowered to offer at this juncture was the bleak prospect of an unspecified period behind barbed wire. Nevertheless, the men were not daunted. In full cognizance of the consequences, they stuck by their decision.

When the totals of the screening process were tabulated, the UNC staff was completely stunned. The victory for voluntary repatriation was overwhelming. Said Colonel Hansen:

"Six thousand nine hundred men, eighty-five percent, forswore their homes and families under Communism; only fifteen percent decided for Red China. And with many of these, it was evident that they reached their decision not because it was Red, but because it was China.

"In the next compound, with more than six thousand occupants, the victory was even more startling. Less than ten percent voted to go home.

"The third compound was a different story. It held only 253 prisoners. They said they were Communists, they were well-organized, and they proved to be Communists. As a man, they elected individually to go to Red China.

"The fourth compound, predominantly Communist but less well

organized, could score only 85% repatriates out of approximately 1500 men.

"The over-all results were four to one, four Chinese who would forcibly resist return to Red China out of each five Chinese prisoners of war. The percentage among the North Koreans only could be estimated, because of the compounds which resisted screening, but in two of the compounds which consented to be screened, the results again exceeded all expectations. In the first, known as the 'Anti-Communist Youth League' Compound, only 18% chose to return to North Korea. The second, the 'Christian Compound,' divided almost equally between repatriation and non-repatriation."

Faithful to Nam Il's orders, the Communist leaders of the North Korean compounds had mobilized fierce resistance to being interrogated and had prevented the entry of UN screening teams. Barred from these "untouchable" compounds, the United Nations Command arrived "by guess and by gosh" at a figure of 70,000 POW's who were willing to accept repatriation:

Civilian internees	7,200
Republic of Korea POW's	3,800
North Korean POW's	53,900
Chinese People's Volunteer POW's	5,100

Even this figure was overly generous, for it included men who were lumped into the total, but who—if screened individually—would probably have elected non-repatriation. The UNC presented these figures with definite forebodings. They were convinced that the Reds would undoubtedly reject them as a case of losing face.

At Panmunjom, the outcome of the screening produced a sensation on the opposite side of the table. "On hearing these results," Admiral Joy reported, "the Communist delegation went through the overhead[2] of the tent.... They charged the United Nations Command with every manner of crime relative to the prisoners. They contended that the screening was done under conditions forcing the prisoners to reject Communism.... Listen for a moment to the voice of our opponents as they raged over our alleged villainy:

GENERAL NAM IL: "Everybody knows that for a long period of time you have been using Chiang Kai-shek's gangsters and Syngman Rhee's agents to take all kinds of barbarous measures to coerce our captured personnel into refusing repatriation. You have not hesitated to use methods of bloodshed and murder to gain your infamous aim. You have not yet made an account for the incidents of February 18th and March 13th, when your side twice massacred our captured personnel."

"In order to assist you to gain the aim of retaining our captured personnel, the Chiang Kai-shek ring repeatedly directed their agents to force our captured personnel to start the so-called movement of refusing repatriation by writing blood petitions, making appeals, and even by announcing collective suicide. For all these facts, our side is in possession of incontestable evidence. Your activities in employing barbarous methods in an attempt to retain our captured personnel by force have already reached such an extent as makes it impossible for your to hide or deny them.

"To strengthen your rule of bloodshed and violence over our captured personnel, your side recently moved large amounts of reinforcing forces to the locality of your prisoner-of-war camp, for further suppression of the just resistance of our captured personnel. The fact now placed before the people of the whole world is that in spite of your such barbarous measures, you violated the will of the captured personnel of our side. Thousands of them would rather die than yield to your forcible retention. Your side dares not face this fact. In order to cover up this fact, your side has invented the myth that our captured personnel were not willing to be repatriated."

More of this uninspired Communist mendacity and vituperation—much more—was in store for the United Nations negotiators. Although no one on the UN staff could have guessed it, nearly a year and a half still separated them from an armistice agreement with the Reds. The main stumbling block in the truce proceedings had now been reached.

In addition to the POW exchange dispute, there were two further points of controversy between the United Nations staff and the Communist delegation. One involved the composition of the so-called Neutral Nations Supervisory Commission—the administrative which would bear the responsibility, in the event that negotiations proved successful, of policing the terms of the armistice agreement. Thus far the Reds had obstinately insisted on nominating the USSR as a "neutral" candidate. For obvious reasons, we had just as obstinately refused to hear of such a proposal, and had offered Norway as an acceptable alternative.

The other, more serious, issue was the matter of airfield construction during the truce. Under no circumstances were we about to permit the Communists to use a cease-fire agreement for the rehabilitation of North Korean airfields and the construction of new forward airstrips as bases for the deployment of Russian-built MIG's. Until or unless some satisfactory arrangements for inspection were reached—we argued—we would be foolish to present the Communists with a priceless opportunity to reinforce their aerial defenses, freed from any concern over attacks by the air forces of the UN.

According to Admiral Joy, there were three ways to resolve these issues: either one side should make concessions on all issues, or both sides should make concessions on all issues, or each side should concede on some issues. He stated categorically that the UNC was not prepared to concede on all issues, and warned the Communists that they must join in some compromise solution or else assume the responsibility for sandbagging the truce negotiations. On April 28, 1952, he submitted the United Nations Command's "package proposal:"

> "In the interest of reaching an early armistice agreement, we are willing to accede to your stand that no restriction be placed on the rehabilitation and construction of airfields. I must make it absolutely clear, however, that our acceptance of your position regarding airfields is contingent upon your accepance of our positions regarding prisoners of war (i.e., voluntary repatriation) and the composition of the Neutral Nations Supervisory Commission (i.e., omission of Norway and the USSR, thus leaving Poland, Czechoslovakia, Sweden and Switzerland)... I wish to emphasize that the United Nations Command offer... is our final and irrevocable effort."

The Communists promptly waved aside this olive branch. Their scornful rejection of our most serious efforts at conciliation to date elicited a dignified but determined rebuttal from the Supreme Commander of the United Nations forces, General Ridgway: "The issues are clear; the stakes are manifest. Our position is one from which we cannot and shall not retreat."

At Koje-do, Nam Il's latest instructions had been received. Earlier orders which enjoined the compound leaders to foment disturbances among the POW's were supplemented by newer directives calling for the seizure of United Nations camp personnel—preferably officers of high rank. Nor did the Communists shrink from the prospect of retaliation. Indeed, they welcomed the possibility of bloody reprisals: the slaughter of a couple of hundred "martyrs" would provide the

Red propaganda apparatus with fresh fuel. According to their view, the POW's were still combatants with nothing to lose but their lives—and these were "for liberation and glorious victory."

The stage was all set for the Dodd drama; the scenario was in the hands of the principals.

It is time now to step behind the scenes and get a closeup of the Communist members of the cast...

CHAPTER TWO

The Face of the Enemy

I'm looking over
A well fought-over
KOREA that I abhor...
anonymous G.I. BALLAD

DURING THE HOT, DUSTY, DESPERATE WEEKS that followed the fall of Seoul, two American newsmen—according to the Far Eastern correspondent, Keyes Beech—halted their jeep at a river crossing to sweat out the passage of oncoming traffic:

"At the side of the road, oblivious to the movement about him, a Korean child was crying as if his heart were broken. He wept freely, without restraint, pouring out his grief in shining tears that coursed down his cheeks to make muddy rivulets in his coat of dust.

'I wonder what he's crying for,' one of the newspapermen said speculatively.

'Because he's a Korean,' said the other, gunning his motor to drown out the child's wailing. 'Isn't that enough?' "

To which every American soldier stationed in Korea would have added a fervent and heartfelt "Amen!" It is probably safe to state that no captive nation throughout history has ever engendered livelier feelings of repugnance among the members of an army of liberation than Korea inspired in the ranks of the U. S. Army. Korea, said Robert T. Oliver in a towering masterpiece of understatement, has not been one of our most popular wars:

> "There is no question that the almost half-million Americans who have fought in the battle of Korea have done so without notable enthusiasm or conviction. Their spirit was pretty well caught by the MP's who devised an effective highway safety sign for the narrow mountain roads: 'Drive carefully. The man you kill may be your replacement.' War is never pretty. In Korea it has been compounded, fractured and obfuscated hell."

Ex-GI's who served in Europe during World War II have sometimes expressed a nostalgic desire to return as a tourist to some of the places they saw first from the rear of a deuce-and-a-half truck or the turret of a Sherman tank. Even veterans of the South Pacific have been known to wonder aloud whether those tropical islands under the wind might manage to live up to their prewar Dotty Lamour reputation without a horde of armed Japanese die-hards for co-tenants.

No ex-GI, however, has ever shown the least inclination toward paying a repeat visit to Korea. The most beautiful view in Korea, as far as most Americans were concerned, was the sight of the Korean coastline receding behind the taffrail of a troop transport bound for Golden Gate.

Such attitudes were by no means confined to homesick GI's suffering the throes of "rotation fever" in a bunker up on the line. Sophisticated timeservers in the *corps diplomatique*, back in those palmier days before the war, resented their exile to this Asian annex of Golgotha; and, among themselves, referred to Korea as "The Land of the Morning Calm, Afternoon Demonstrations, and Nightsoil." Some two-star panjandrum in the British contingent once snorted into his whiskey-and-water and loudly lamented: "What can you do with a place that doesn't have a single golf course in the whole bloody country, and has a prime minister named Lee Bum Suk?"

But rejection of Korea and things Korean goes back even further than the Truman Doctrine and the Marshall Plan. When Terry compiled his tourist "guide to the Japanese Empire" just before World War I, he dipped his pen in vitriol for a dissertation on Korea:

> "The native villages are little better than those of Hottentots—pictures of filth, poverty, and sloth. Many of the huts are round and straw, and so poor that 20 *yen* in cash would buy a town.[1] The dead level of poverty is everywhere apparent. Lines of dirty men and women with a dazed and purposeless air travel between these spots and the adjacent fields, where red cattle help to drag rude ploughs inferior to those used in Pharaoh's time, and aid in methods of irrigation (necessary only for the rice-fields), that suggest Biblical epochs. One occasionally sees men making visible efforts to work clad only in a fillet bound round the head; others waste the precious hours strutting about smoking contemptible little long-stemmed pipes in an effort to fill their monotonous lives in a monotonous region. The villages are usually attended by a retinue of voluminously clad, bare-breasted women destitute of grace and pulchritude; by squalid children, black goats, runty black pigs of revolting habits, and noisy geese, the latter kept chiefly as guards and for presentation at weddings as emblems of fidelity,—something the Koreans do not possess."

Terry could have found no quarrel with the American soldier who summed up his impressions of Korea by the terse statement: "Take all the worse features of every country, put them together, and you'll have Korea." Except that Terry would have insisted, no doubt, that the formula ought to be extended to include Koreans, as well:

> "In many respects the Korean is *sui generis*. Frugal in the use of

water (to which he has a determined hostility), fond of a frowsy smell, economical of the truth, as avid of 'fire-water' as the red man of the American plains, and with light prehensile fingers that readily assimilate the detachable impedimenta of the 'foreign devil,' he suspects the wide world and possesses to a sordid degree the Oriental vices of duplicity, cunning, and general untrustworthiness. He steals freely when the opportunity offers, and his capacious sleeves and balloon-like trousers make ideal places of concealment for one's cherished belongings. The spawn of a low order of civilization, he is untidy and swinish in his habits, and apathetic in the face of work—for which he has a fervid distaste. He is a born dawdler, gambler, and brawler: and, like the Chinaman, he has, in his fathomless conceit and besotted ignorance, a sturdy and unshakable faith in his own impeccability and the flagrant worthlessness of everything foreign. He is lethargic, purposeless, devoid of thrift or ambition, and he dwells contentedly amidst incredible dirt and discomfort. His specialty—the curse of his country—is sorning on his relatives or friends. He is an inveterate smoker and he will sit for hours in a limp state of fatuous vacuity, sucking a bowlful of tobacco not larger than a marrowfat pea, while his puny wife (or one of several concubines)—usually several hands shorter and of much smaller physique—may be squatting beside some wayside pool washing the raiment which her lord and master always wears out first in the seat..."

Nature, climate, geography, power politics—together with Fate—ganged up and handed Korea and the Koreans a raw deal. One need merely glance at a map to comprehend the reason for a large part of the Korean tragedy. For four thousand years, Korea has been cursed by its strategic location. Said Robert T. Oliver:

"An image that has become vivid in our imaginations is the old Roman custom at gladiatorial contests of turning thumbs up or thumbs down to signal life or death for the fallen gladiator who lies with his victor's sword point on his throat. This image is worth recalling in connection with a contemporary description of Korea as 'The thumb of Asia.'... The thumb is a pictorial image for Korea if only because of its size, shape, and the angle at which it projects from the great fist of continental Asia... The thumb is the fulcrum of the hand. If the thumb is injured, the whole hand loses its power. A paralyzed or amputated thumb means a practically helpless hand. The thumb is far from lovely and never the inspiration for poetic rhapsody, but by the test of practicality, it is essential."

As a consequence of its geographical position, Oliver points out, Korea was predestined to serve in the principal role of buffer state: "Never strong militarily and never ambitious for expansion, Korea in itself has not been a threat to anyone. Its significance lies now (as it has in the past) in the fact that it occupies the strategic heartland of north Asia, surrounded by China, Japan, and Siberian Russia. So long as Korea is truly independent, these powers are kept apart and the peace of Asia is safe. As soon as Korea is dominated by one of them, the other two are endangered. This a truism impossible to avoid."

Circumstances such as these have shaped the national character of Korea through forty centuries of dark, turbulent history, and left their indelible imprint upon the Korean people. Walled off during its earliest existence from close contact with the other peoples of Asia—by Pakdusan, the Everwhite Mountain, and the swift-flowing Tumen and Yalu Rivers to the north, and by the sea on the three remaining sides—there was an inevitable tendency toward the development of national traits of introversion. Isolation led to the slow accretion of customs indigenous to Korea and duplicated nowhere else in the world. Korea, even then, was a Hermit Kingdom.

But this peaceful solitude was shattered irrevocably when population pressures, imperialist designs, or a thirst for freebootery drove the Chinese and the Japanese into fierce contention for possession of this strategic area:

> "Across the Straits of Korea to the South lay the land of the Ainu warriors, the pirates, the warlords who swooped down on their shores only to raid, burn and steal. Up to the north were the fierce Manchus, and during the disturbed twelfth and thirteenth centuries the ruthlessly murdering Tartar hordes of Ghengis Khan... 'Shut them out!' was the remedy adopted by the peace-loving inhabitants of Old Korea. Especially after the searing blight of the Hideyoshi invasion, the Koreans sought to build a wall around their country to keep out foreigners who came only to despoil and steal. Then it was that Korea became The Hermit Kingdom, a forbidden land."

Back and forth over the length and breadth of the peninsula, the deadly comb of bloody oppression and subjugation has raked, since time out of mind. No country in the world has known the hell of the conqueror as often as Korea. Hatred and distrust of foreigners—indeed, of anything foreign—has therefore at times assumed the status of a religion with the Koreans. A missionary who traveled to Korea in the 1890's found weathered stone tablets standing at the roadsides which bore a message: "If you meet a foreigner kill him; he who lets him go by is a traitor to his country."

The very name Koreans gave their country was indicative of their deep-seated instinctual desire to be left alone, unmolested. As late as the last quarter of the 19th century, it was possible to find a commentary like this one: "It is not an exaggeration to say that geographers know more of central Africa and its mountain and river systems than they do of the interior of this mere promontory, interposed like a wedge between the seas of China and Japan."

Periods of isolation have often been for the Koreans, like the convalescent period for the invalid, a time of burgeoning prosperity and a renaissance in cultural and political activities. During its long 500-year rule, the Yi dynasty—which remained in power until Korea was annexed by the Japanese in 1910—has known several such "eras of good feeling." According to McCune: "The first, occurring in the opening years of the fourteenth century, was probably the greatest. At that time an alphabet was invented which was admirably suited to the Korean language, movable metal type was developed (at least fifty years before Gutenberg), encyclopedias and histories were written, and good government established according to the strictest of Confucian principles...

"Two hundred years after the establishment of the dynasty, the Japanese invasion of 1592 put an end to the prosperity of the country, but seven years of conflict resulted in the withdrawal of Japanese troops and the abandonment of Hideyoshi's plan of conquest. One cause of the Japanese retreat was the brilliant naval victories of Admiral Yi Sunsin, who invented the iron-clad turtle ship which he directed with such superior strategy that he was able to break the strength of the Japanese navy."

In later years, however, Korea's self-imposed isolation was decidedly to her detriment. By fending off all contacts with the outside world, by attacking and burning the occasional Western ships that sought haven in one of her numerous harbors, by persecuting and killing the few missionaries who presumed to venture upon their jealously-guarded soil, the Koreans stopped the clock of material progress somewhere in the middle ages. The industrial revolution passed them by imperceptibly.

Not until 1882 did Korea remove the stubborn barriers to intercourse with the rest of the world that had been erected during the Yi dynasty—and then it was only because Japanese pressures to do so proved impossible to resist. To some observers, it seemed that Japanese domination was a blessing in disguise for the Koreans whose society, according to Isabella Bishop, was staggering under "... a total absence of justice, the insecurity of all earnings, a government which has carried out the worst traditions on which all Oriental Governments are based, a class of official robbers steeped in intrigue, a monarch enfeebled by the seclusion of the palace seraglio, the mutual jealousies of interested foreigners, and an all-pervading and terrorizing superstition."[2]

By a coincidence which seems almost fateful, the first nation of the West to conclude a treaty with Korea was, oddly, the United States.

Korea is a bleak and forbidding country.

Nature has never seen fit to lavish many gifts on this rugged peninsula. Long after every other impression of Korea has faded, the visitor remembers the hills—as eroded and fissured as an old man's cheeks. *San way you san san pool chin* is the way the Koreans themselves describe their country: "Over the hills, hills again, hills without number." Or, in the words of an American correspondent, "Just one damned hill after another."

The influence of physical environment on personality is a matter that psychologists are still debating in their professional journals. Nevertheless, it seems difficult to deny that existence in a harsh, barren land is not conducive to the development of the softer virtues. And some of the conditions normal to life in Korea would make an ancient Spartan upbringing seem like a sybaritic wallowing in sinful luxury, by comparison. Man for man, woman for woman, the Koreans are probably the toughest human species in the world. There is no such thing as a Korean weakling. They were long since bred out of the race; only the hardiest have survived.

By Western—and particularly American—standards, the Koreans seem queer and unappealing. Debased by centuries of cruel oppression, their faces are usually devoid of expression and animation; the inevitable result of being compelled to mask one's feelings from the hated conqueror. As John Dille notes:

"Living on a narrow, rocky, and vulnerable appendage to Asia has given the Koreans a tremendous feeling of insecurity. And their long centuries of complete subjugation, to Chinese invaders or Japanese conquerors, have so deprived them of political maturity and material progress that their sense of inferiority often reaches the level of complete self-deprecation. Koreans are also a frank and direct people. After watching them shove each other around in the market place, after seeing their youngsters play their ruthless game with rocks—in which the point of the game is to bring blood—and after learning of their standard procedure for discipline in the army —a severe beating or hefty slaps in the face—one gets the impression that they dislike themselves almost as much as other people do.

"Strangely enough, the net result of this lack of group humanity and charity toward one another seems to be a feeling of personal self-reliance and individual pride which would have done Emerson's heart good...

"The Koreans do not bow and scrape and disarm their acquaintances with a wide, saccharine smile as do some Orientals. They are almost cold and haughty in their pride."

Relations between the sexes in Korea—at least until the outbreak of the Korean war—were customarily austere to the point of icy formality. Marriages were arranged by the respective families, with no nonsense about romance. The Korean moral code, Dille observes, is probably one of the most puritanical in the world:

"And unlike the American code, it is adhered to strictly. Virginity, among both men and women, is common. Social dancing is prohibited by law as unseemly. And before a movie can be shown in a Korean theater it is supposed to be trimmed first of all kissing scenes—a rule which naturally makes mincemeat of many an American import.

"The Koreans themselves do not kiss in public, and they would rather not see other people doing it. Their love-making, in fact, is about as staid and unadorned by displays of emotion and affection —even in private—as it is possible for love-making to get...

"Even when a Korean and his wife or fiancée had been separated by the war for several months, it was not unusual, upon their reunion, for them to greet each other solemnly and sedately on the street, exactly as if they were passing acquaintances who had already passed on the street three times before on the same morning. There was no visible emotion..."

But this is only one side of the Korean character.

That placid, serene surface turns out to be a mere lid, held on precariously at the best of times, over the pressurized vessel of Korean temper. Not without reason have the Koreans been dubbed the "Irish of the Orient." Unlike the more emotionally inhibited Japanese, their feelings are at all times close to the surface. "Their tempers," says Keyes Beech, "are as hot as their peppery foods, as savage as their shaggy, nasty-tempered ponies. They like to throw rocks at one another, often with fatal results. They riot with the suddenness of a summer squall, and just as quickly subside. The Korean's willingness to fight at the drop of a hat is supported by legend. According to legend, the Korean's tall, delicately fashioned hat was first made of porcelain, in the hope that possible loss of so valuable an item would discourage him from fighting."

Some sociologists, on the other hand, maintain that the Koreans are more like the "rugged, temperamental natives of the cold Russian steppes than like any other nearby race," according to John Dille. "In the long, freezing winters they seem to store up their temper and exuberance, like a tiger in hibernation. Then, when spring comes, they explode with violent arguments and fatal stone fights."

Nor are Korean women exempt from these volatile personality characteristics. Like one of Kipling's she-bears, the female is more to be feared than the male. One of the most unflattering portraits in Terry's gallery is this rough sketch of the Korean woman:

> "As a rule they are ill-bred and unmannerly, far removed from the gracefulness and charm of the same class in Japan. The wearing of white clothes by the men puts severe and almost incessant work on the women's shoulders, and they are the national drudges. They have few if any pleasures, and they try to get even with fate by singeing their compatriots with the lash of their pungent and scarifying vocabulary. The average low-class women possess a fund of invective that usually sends the men scattering to the four points of the compass; it is as inelegant as it is complete, and it seems to be both dreaded and effective. Age treats these poor creatures shockingly; at 30 they look 50, and at 60 the stranger wishes he hadn't seen them. Their vixenish dispositions indubitably add to their extraordinary unattractiveness."

On a more up-to-date note, there is William L. White's description of the feminine POW's we repatriated in "Operation Big Switch" at Panmunjom:

> "Among our returnees were several hundred North Korean WAC's, and, once loaded into the railway car where they knew they could not be tear-gassed, these merry Marxist minxes proceeded to show their dainty disdain for all things capitalist by tidily turning it into a shambles.

"First they smashed every window in every coach. Then they slashed the seat coverings with razor blades. Thirdly, climbing up on the seats, blithely they urinated into the upholstery. Finally, and just before leaving the train, militantly and definitively they defecated in the aisles."

Our soldiers who were unfortunate enough to experience captivity under both the North Koreans and the Chinese—those who managed to survive their treatment at the hands of the former—are unanimous in affirming that the cruelty and brutality of their Korean captors far exceeded anything they received from the Chinese. Prisoner after prisoner, Keyes Beech stated, reported that his treatment, "while it still left a great deal to be desired, improved almost overnight when he was transferred from North Korean to Chinese custody."

Soldiers of the 24th Infantry Division who participated in the 1950 "Death March" tell of the scar-faced North Korean murderer called "The Killer" who shot 28 men for the least infraction of the rules, or merely because they were too weak to continue.

American fliers were especially singled out for cruel treatment by the North Koreans. Their cruelty, Beech suggests, was the primitive, irrational hatred of the Korean toward the ones he held responsible for the destruction of his homes, his villages, and his cities by American aircraft. Until the Chinese intervened to make use of American aviators for propaganda purposes in eliciting "confessions" of germ-warfare, most American fliers were simply tortured, then shot out of hand.

As one GI put it, "The Koreans, they always used force to get what they wanted. The Chinese used psych." He did not mean by this to imply that the Red Chinese were motivated by any loftier, altruistic aims than their North Korean colleagues. It was merely that the Chinese—an eminently practical people—were well aware of the difficulties involved in extracting any propaganda value from an American corpse. With captured ROK soldiers, on the other hand, they were far less restrained.

These were the prisoners, then, who jammed the UN camp at Koje-do—over 100,000 of them. Men of hardy peasant stock, inured by a life of hardship and privation in a harsh, pitiless land; men to whom brutality was a commonplace of daily existence, who were accustomed to cruelty as one of the immutabilities of life; by nature bellicose and given to sullen, brooding resentment and sudden outbursts of savage temper. It is to these characteristics of the Korean personality that one must look first in seeking an explanation of the insurrections at Koje-do. Even without the yeasty ferment of political agitation and the disruptive element of Red fanaticism, the mere act of incarcerating more than 100,000 men bred to a rugged individualism would have posed some knotty problems for any Koje-do commander.

This was the first step—as Generals Dodd and Colson had to learn the hard way—in a flight of stairs that led downward into mutiny, violence, and bloodshed.

CHAPTER THREE

Morning Calm & Rising Storm

TWENTY MILES BY FERRY from the cluttered docks of Pusan is the island of Koje—an irregular-shaped blob of land about 150 square miles in size which shelters the pleasant bay of Chinhae. Twice that distance to the southeast, across the Korean Straits, lies the Japanese island of Tsushima, scene of a previous clash between the Orient and the Occident. It was in these waters, back in 1905, that the newly created naval might of the Japanese Empire, under the command of Admiral Togo, met the Russian fleet.

For an American stationed on Koje-do in 1952, a passing acquaintance with Far Eastern history might have provided the material for some intriguing reflections on the vagaries of international politics. In that earlier conflict, the armed forces of reactionary Czarist Russia were pitted against the rising power of Asia's first nation to cross the feudal threshold into modernity. Now, almost a half-century later, a revolutionary Russia backed the claims of another emergent Asian nation against the much-propagandized "Wall Street imperialists." Today's struggle was one of ideologies in which the issues had all but effaced the natural contours of race, economics, and geography.

Some bleak comfort, however, might have been drawn from the fact that the Russians sustained a resounding defeat in that naval engagement fought not far from the island of Koje.

On the western side of Koje-do, the coast is rocky, precipitous, and deeply indented; but, to the east and south, the shoreline is hospitable to small fishing craft.

Inland, the terrain is a faithful replica of the Korean peninsula: steep, barren hills covered with scraggly brush and granite outcroppings; and fertile valleys zigzagged with small embankments which separate one patch of rice-paddy from another. These neat dikes march in serried ranks right up the lower slopes where they break step and scatter into a profusion of small, terraced enclosures.

The alluvial plains are waist-deep with a rich, black humus that has been made even richer by centuries of impregnation with human dung—a practice which announces itself to the nostrils without benefit of even a desultory breeze. Rice is the staple crop, but smaller parcels of the precious soil are given over to the cultivation of Chinese cabbage, *daikon*—a species of large, bland radish—soybeans, wheat, and barley. With the addition of fish and seafood taken in shoal waters by skillful fishermen, these crops provided an austere existence before the war for 50,000 Koje Islanders—people who are as rugged and durable as their harsh surroundings.

Koje is dotted with clusters of mud-daub and thatched roof huts, but few of these settlements are large enough to deserve the name of town. Changsungpo and Chuktori—villages in the south and north, respectively—are the closest thing to a town that Koje-do can boast.

The choice of such a remote and unpromising location for a POW camp was determined partly by desirability and partly by necessity. According to General Mark Clark:

> "The prisoner problem became acute for the United Nations Command in late 1950 after the Chinese Communists were hurled across the Yalu and into the war in Korea. Victory over the North Korean army had left 100,000 Communist POW's in Allied hands. In the withdrawals before the great mass of Chinese troops the

> United Nations had to evacuate these prisoners from their well-dispersed prison camps and to concentrate them in the area of Pusan, on the southern tip of Korea. There the large number of prisoners, plus the far greater number of refugees, became a major barrier to the smooth movement of supplies for Allied troops. It was decided to establish a POW installation on the island of Koje, large enough to accommodate the entire mass of Communist prisoners and close enough to the Korean coast for relatively easy transport."

Colonel Kenneth Hansen offers an additional reason: "They were placed on Koje Island... so that in the event of UNC reverses and organized action on the prisoners' part there would be at least a stretch of water between them and the Eighth Army's rear."

In terms of physical layout, the camp consisted of four barbed wire enclosures, each divided into eight compounds. A single compound was designed to hold up to 6,000 prisoners. (There seems to have been little recognition at this time of the dangers involved in such large concentrations of enemy captives.) In deference to the needs of the Koje Islanders, the United Nations Command selected the campsites from barren, rock-strewn hillsides and plateaus—to avoid using up land that was suitable for farming.

Prisoners were housed, at first, in tents, and these were winterized as rapidly as materials became available. Later, when the camp was well-established, permanent buildings were added. The efforts of the prisoners themselves—especially in anti-Communist compounds—contributed greatly to making the camp comfortable and habitable.

Initial construction began in the early months of 1951. By the middle of the year there were 130,000 Koreans and 20,000 Chinese on Koje-do. Heavy fighting in the spring of 1951 had swollen the ranks of the prisoners.

When Swiss representatives from the International Red Cross visited the UN camps at Pusan and Koje-do in the late summer of 1951, they were quite favorably impressed by what they saw. As they stated in their official report, the POW's were quartered in compounds which had "reached almost the maximum state of perfection in layout, decoration, cleanliness." The report also mentioned that the prisoners received exactly the same daily rations as those issued to UNC personnel.

A visit to Compound 72, which housed Chinese officers, proved diverting to the gentlemen from Geneva. They found it "an extraordinary sight with picturesque pagodas, arches to feeding lines, tent decorations (nearly all made with discarded tin cans), life-sized clay figures and ground decorations made with colored clay." Morale, they reported, was excellent. Nobody was idle, and prisoners "were observed polishing the clay walls around the tents, while others kept the ground decorations of small pebbles in order."

The prisoners had no complaints to make.

"Each week a committee of UN officers...decides which is the 'Best Compound of the Week.' The winning compound receives a plaque, which is proudly displayed over the entrance."

But all was not sweetness and light in the POW camps. On V-J Day, which is celebrated in both North and South Korea as Independence Day, there occurred a serious outbreak of violence in the Pusan camp which forecast the ominous shape of succeeding developments at Koje-do.

The camp commandant at Pusan, having received information that trouble was brewing, had doubled the ROK guard details. Political leaflets, presumably smuggled in by POW nurses, had been distributed throughout the camp. They were of both Communist and anti-Communist origin—and the latter were mimeographed on paper that apparently came from United Nations supply.

As evening approached, the tension within the camp rapidly mounted. Every prisoner was outside his quarters in the assembly area milling about restlessly and listening to exhortations from fellow prisoners. Compound after compound broke into roaring political song and, with linked arms, paraded or snake-danced through the enclosure.

The guards began to grow uneasy. Prisoners surged in masses against the barbed wire fences shouting insults at their captors. A direct order to the POW's in Compound 11 to withdraw to their tents was ignored.

It was 2215 hours—10:15 p.m.

All at once a shower of rocks burst from the enclosures. Some were hurled at the guards, others were thrown at nearby compounds which quartered "the enemy"—anti-Communist prisoners to the fanatical Reds, and vice versa.

At 2230 hours the guards—now apprehensive of mass escape attempts—moved in to try and get the situation under control. Some of the ROK soldiers fired warning shots in the air; others directly at the shouting, pushing, rockthrowing mob of prisoners.

The outbreak subsided as quickly as it had begun, but six prisoners had been killed and 24 had been wounded. Of these, 3 later died.

Independence Day had also brought death and bloodshed to Koje-do. In Compound 65, another enclosure that was rent with factionalism among the POW's, there had been a clash between the prisoners and their guards earlier in the evening. After the disturbance had been suppressed, violence flared up again between the prisoners themselves. Later that night, a group of anti-Communist prisoners overpowered their compound guards—POW's who operated as a goon squad for the Red bosses of the enclosure—and gave them a stiff going-over. Towards morning, however, with the help of reinforcements, the guards returned and jumped the prisoners who had roughed them up earlier. They exacted their revenge by meting out savage punishment to their attackers.

The casualties from this donnybrook were as heavy as those sustained in the Pusan riots: 3 killed and 26 injured. But they were all incurred as a result of the struggle among the prisoners themselves within the camp. No UN guards were involved in this affair.

The Red Cross reported that "These incidents have caused the Detaining Power great concern. A Board of Officers is investigating." Many of the ROK soldiers, the report mentioned, were young and inexperienced; and the UNC, according to the Swiss, was considering their replacement.

But it would take much more than the transfer of a few trigger-happy ROK guards to bring order to the teeming compounds at Koje-do. There was, for example, the matter of the mutilated corpses that turned up every few mornings at the gates to some compounds. What motives were behind these murders? Were they killings in settlement of private grudges?

It was hard to find out. Nobody was talking—at least, not to their captors. But it was clear that something more than private vengeance was involved in these bloody assassinations.

Koje camp was a huge tank; and the great mass of Korean and Chinese prisoners was like some vast electrolytic bath in which a process of polarization was at work. Anode—Communism; cathode—anti-Communism. The sporadic riots that had roiled the surface thus far were merely bubbles breaking; the real agitation was down below. Until recently, the Swiss report noted, it had been "possible to guard the POW with a minimum of personnel." But how, "under present circumstances the prisoners are excitable, unstable, and restless."

Among the terms of the Geneva Convention is one which has to do with the election of compound spokesmen. These men are entrusted with the task of providing representation for their fellow POW's with the camp commandant and his staff: conveying requests, registering grievances, helping in the maintenance of discipline and standards of cleanliness, and upholding the rights of the prisoners. In turn, they transmit orders from the commandant and operate as a channel of communication between the camp authorities and the POW's.

It was increasingly apparent, however, that the violent political pressures building up at Koje had distorted the role of the spokesman out of all resemblance to what was specified in the Geneva Conventions. Spokesmen were less concerned about protecting prisoners' rights than in serving the Communist or anti-Communist faction which had put them in office. "What seemed to be taking place here," said William L. White, "was that in some compounds the prisoners, perhaps fed up with Communists, had chosen others. So the Communists were fighting to regain control. In other compounds, prisoners had elected not the ranking officer, but the ranking Communist political agitator. He and his gang had taken over and were ruthlessly purging all opposition."

The Swiss report stated that "in spite of secret ballots, very few elections produce persons capable of carrying out the tasks mentioned in the Conventions." The report mentioned one spokesman who had just been elected, but whose immediate removal was necessary: he had personally led a group that had mistreated two prisoners. The camp commandant "explained how difficult it is to keep each tent under observation in complete darkness. These beatings (he said) which unfortunately often cause deaths, happen quickly and are carried out by well-organized groups. Even should the culprit be recognized by tent inmates, fear prevents witnesses from giving evidence."Neither faction was ready to include the UN in its confidence. Said White:

"Often the elected spokesman was only a figure-head. A little Korean with the humblest task in the camp might be the real boss-man.

"But why should we interfere? So long as we followed Geneva and fed our former foes well, what difference did it make to us if they found political murder a more exciting sport than volleyball?

"The trouble was, we had to act. Because right there in the Book (Geneva Conventions 1949, Article 121) we could be held responsible for the 'death or serious injury' of any POW, even if caused by 'another Prisoner of War.'

"Clearly we must do something. Because if we failed to keep them from bashing in one another's skulls, Geneva could hold us responsible. Yet could we legally separate political factions? Back now to the book, where Geneva's Article 16 says:

'ALL PRISONERS OF WAR WILL BE TREATED ALIKE BY THE DETAINING POWER WITHOUT ADVERSE DISTINCTION BASED ON RACE, NATIONALITY, RELIGIOUS BELIEF OR POLITICAL OPINION...'

"Read together, the two articles meant that if we failed to segregate, we would be responsible for the deaths, but each faction must get equal treatment. We now went about the delicate task of pulling them apart. It was not easy. Communist political agitators resisted being plucked from what in their terms were disloyal compounds. It was their duty to stay on and regain control.

"As for us—the American captors—few then realized that we soon were to have the painful task of umpiring an important part of Korea's Civil War, which, revived by our good food, was to rise in our POW camps. It was, for the moment, our duty only to put a stop to those mangled corpses which appeared at the compound gates, before the neutral Swiss could protest. Let these North Koreans fight it out after they got back home, we said."

All these fever symptoms were also evident in the normally docile Chinese POW's. On November 2, 1951, Red Cross representative Otto Lehner had occasion to inform the United Nations Command Headquarters in Tokyo:

"I have received 3 petitions from a number of Chinese Prisoners of War who are anxious not to be repatriated... The International Red Cross is not, I feel, in a position to express considered opinions... since political considerations lie wholly outside its terms of reference.

"However...the International Red Cross...could be led, on the grounds of concrete facts consequent on decisions taken by the responsible Authorities...to make this its concern...in conformity with its traditional policy of protection for Prisoners of War."

"Behind this cautious language," White observed, "it is clear that already Lehner and the other neutral Swiss could see that violent political differences among the prisoners might lead many to resist return to their Communist homelands. He now hints that the International Red Cross might handle the necessary screening if asked to do this by both sides."

As winter approached, the alarums and excursions of autumn appeared to have subsided. Red Cross Delegate Frederick Bieri poked his head into one of the compounds that housed North Korean officers —fanatical, hard-core Communists to a man—and found nothing more violent in progress than an impromptu dance session, with five "couples" waltzing to the strains of "The Merry Widow" played on a harmonica by one of the other prisoners. Senior Colonel Lee, the compound spokesman—about whom more shall be heard later—

informed Bieri that "cooperation with the Detaining Power was good" and that neither he nor his men had any complaints about their treatment.

Delegate Bieri noted approvingly that the POW's in most compounds were taking advantage of the educational and vocational training program that the UN camp authorities had set up.[1] Classrooms were filled; attendance was regular; and there were no hints of trouble.

The lull was deceptive, for it presaged a further outbreak of violence...

Word was passed to the Red Cross that a new camp was under construction on Koje-do. This compound was intended to hold a special group of prisoners: people who had been residents of South Korea at the time the war broke out, but who had been captured in North Korean uniform.

"Behind this announcement," noted William L. White, "lay a tangled tale. According to Colonel R. R. Ramsey, who handled this confusion for the Provost Marshal's office, in the huge bag of prisoners we took just after the Inchon landings some 50,000 swore they were loyal South Koreans, brutally impressed into the Communist armies by the invading North Koreans.

"In most cases this was true. Some, however, were North Korean Communists masquerading as South Koreans, hoping to escape prison camp. Still others had been South Korean Communists who had willingly joined up, but now were pretending they had been shanghaied.

"In the beginning, however, taking their unsupported word, we had tentatively classified them as Civilian Internees. But we had asked President Syngman Rhee to provide us with screening committees representing every province of Korea, so that each man could be questioned by neighbors who would know how much (if any) of his story was true."

The work dragged on and on. As the completed dossiers piled up, the original figure of 50,000 slowly diminished. But, in the meantime, the vigilant and observant Communists tucked away in the obscurity of this mass of legitimate war victims came to another thoughtful conclusion after watching our methods of operation: namely, that in a stockade run by these guileless Americans, it was not even necessary to conceal one's Communist sympathies in order to receive correct treatment.

In one of these 6,000-man Civilian Internee compounds, the disciplined nucleus of Red leaders—emboldened by American scruples regarding political nonintervention—cast aside further pretense and decisively seized control. After committing a few murders to cow their opponents, they brazenly insisted that Compound 62 should be reclassified as a POW compound. Although every prisoner in the enclosure had been a legal resident of South Korea before 1950, the Communists argued that they were all loyal members of the North Korean Army, and that they expected to be repatriated to North Korea along with the other military prisoners.

Was there any truth at all to these assertions?

The harrassed camp commandant hesitated to say for certain. He knew that there were large numbers of prisoners in Compound 62—at a guess, perhaps as many as fifty percent—whose sentiments were staunchly anti-Communist. But in the face of savage Communist intimidation, these men were understandably reluctant to declare their allegiance to the opposition.

In order to separate the two factions, the camp commander decided to carry out a further screening. Teams of South Koreans were organized to give the prisoners in Compound 62 individual interviews.

Trouble started at once. As soon as the announcements were made, the new Communist bosses of the compound greeted the UN authorities with carefully organized defiance. No screening teams, they insisted, were going to set foot in Compound 62.

American camp officials acted promptly and with firmness. They segregated 17 of the recognized Red leaders in a locked enclosure within the compound and imported 75 anti-Communist civilian internees from a nearby compound to assist the Korean screening teams in maintaining order.

Events, at this point, developed according to what by now was a familiar pattern: on the morning of December 23rd, "pro-and-con singing" of political songs began among the prisoners, milling masses of POW's gathered in the assembly areas, and taunts were hurled at the UN guards. The Communist leaders somehow managed to break out of their makeshift brig and bullied their way to the center of the compound where they rallied their stooges.

The camp commander—"a simple, forthright soldier now dazzled by the subleties of Oriental politics," as White described him—was at a loss to cope with the situation. According to the commandant, "a general uproar followed, in which everybody seemed to be chasing everybody else." Said White:

"The Communist leaders, now back in control, had first turned their attention to the 75 imported anti-Communist Civilian Internees who, now badly scared and with good reason, 'attempted to climb over the fence to escape their aggressors.'

"The ROK guards outside this compound, alarmed by the shindy, seeing men try to escape from the compound and not knowing why, fired, killing four—one of whom had been a fleeing anti-Communist and the others his vengeful pursuers.

"At this point, the American commander, arriving on the battlefield, had taken over. He ordered the ROK guards to fire one shot in the air, as an assertion of authority. He then ordered all prisoners to squat, regardless of politics.

"He informed all these squatters that 'every man who wished to avoid further political complications could leave the compound.' Some 800 instantly took advantage of this, which left the Communist leaders in undisputed control of Compound 62."

There were still undoubtedly a great many frightened anti-Communists behind the barbed wire of Compound 62, but only a thorough screening could cull them out of the militantly defiant Red mass. Meanwhile, the camp commandant informed Red Cross Delegate Bieri, "Compound 62 is to be considered a Communist compound...to which Communist Civilian Internees from other compounds...will be sent" as they were processed by the screening teams.

From the Red leaders of Compound 62, Monsieur Bieri received a quite different version of the December 23rd riot. The fusillade from the ROK guards outside the fence had been "unwarranted and unnecessary," they declared. According to them, the 75 anti-Communist civilians had been brought into their compound "for the express purpose of beating and torturing them." Their chief spokesman demanded that Senior Colonel Lee—spokesman for the solidly Communist North Korean Officer's compound—be allowed to visit them.

Bieri obligingly relayed this demand to the camp authorities, who immediately vetoed it. But Bieri himself paid a visit to Colonel Lee. The Communist grapevine had kept the Colonel fully informed of the events in Compound 62. Lee told Bieri that his only concern, as ranking Communist officer in the camp, was to help keep the prisoners in line. The dastardly Americans, he was now convinced, would never release the civilians in Compound 62 to return to North Korea.

Throughout the whole Koje complex, in each compound, the voluntary repatriation issue was being fought out to the last desperate inch. Depending on how the struggle swayed, prisoners were electing new compound spokesmen and deposing old ones—sometimes Communist, sometimes anti-Communist.

According to White, little of importance escaped the watchful eye of Swiss Delegate Bieri:

"Passing one Korean POW compound, he was surprised to find 'a few hundred prisoners squatting in orderly rows in front of the exit' and learned that they were 'the former spokesman's favorites... They were now frightened of reprisals from the "new party" and desired to transfer to another compound.'

"The Chinese prisoners were also restless, and in one compound a colonel wanted permission to visit two other Chinese compounds because, as he told Bieri, he was 'very much concerned about the political situation there.' On the question of whether or not they should go to Formosa after the war, the colonel feared that 'pressure is being applied amongst the POW themselves.'

"The Chinese colonel, although loyal to his Communist government, 'recognized that some POW's desire to go to Formosa but would, in the interests of a "peaceful life," like to see a strict division made between the two factions'."

It is fortunate that the busy gentleman from Geneva somehow found time amidst his travels to compose a report on the political situation in the United Nations prisoner of war camps. After visiting compounds 9 and 10 on the mainland near Pusan, Delegate Bieri wrote a detailed summary which covered developments up through January 16, 1952. At a much later date, when the anti-Communist prisoners who had rejected repatriation were being held in custody by the neutral Indians near Panmunjom, the Reds charged that they had been subjected to intimidation from strong-arm squads acting on orders from "the puppet Rhee," or terrorists dispatched from Formosa by "the bandit Chiang." Two years before they were made, these absurd charges were effectively refuted by Delegate Bieri's January, 1952 report:

> "...in spite of their personal worries concerning repatriation, the majority of the prisoners seem to be content. The (American) Camp authorities are doing their best to keep 'political peace' inside the compounds.
>
> "Many spokesmen have informed the Delegate of their grave concern over repatriation.
>
> "There are North and South Koreans (both Prisoners and Civilian Internees) who wish to return to North Korea.
>
> "There are North and South Koreans (both Prisoners and Civilian Internees) who desire to remain in South Korea.
>
> "Many men at present living in close contact with those of opposite ideologies are scared to express their real opinion.
>
> "Others have been forced by their comrades to make statements which are contrary to their wishes.
>
> "The effects of political pressure from both sides, as applied by the prisoners themselves, can be clearly observed."

A fair and thorough screening, as Delegate Lehner had suggested earlier, seemed the only solution to this unfortunate situation. But a fair and thorough screening was the last thing in the world the Communists were ready to accept.

In early February, the Communists who had wrested control of Compound 62—the turbulent enclosure that housed the erstwhile Civilian Internees—requested permission from the Koje authorities to celebrate the anniversary of the founding of the North Korean Army.

Despite the fact that each and every inmate of the compound had once sworn he was a loyal anti-Communist South Korean, the Red leaders now swore that all the prisoners were staunchly loyal members of the North Korean Army.

For unmitigated gall this latest piece of Communist arrogance was in a class by itself. It is all the more shocking to learn that the event was observed in that compound "with Communist speeches, banners and songs," by the indulgence of the U.S. camp authorities. "To an American alumnus of Communist-run prison camps on the Yalu," White remarked, "this degree of political freedom will seem fantastic. It would have been unthinkable for their Chinese wardens to allow an American flag, song or patriotic speech."

The day after the gala Red fête, Red Cross Delegate Lehner dropped around to Compound 62 and found the Communist spokesmen whipping up the internees to resist the proposed rescreening:

> "On this point the delegate tried to argue, pointing out that since each one had once signed a document swearing he was a loyal South Korean who desired to remain in that country, it was not unreasonable for the Americans now to ask each if he had changed his mind.
>
> "Firmly, the spokesman told him that the men would not allow it. They were, he insisted, unanimously pro-Communist, and pressure had been brought on them in the first screening. The spokesman also complained that men from anti-Communist Korean compounds, passing theirs, had chucked rocks into it. The Americans also had had the effrontery to ask them to take down their Communist flags, now that the celebration was over.
>
> "Obediently, the neutral Swiss went away to transmit these complaints and declarations to the American commander. Re-

turning, he told the Communist spokesman that the Americans had said the banners and decorations should be taken down.

"Whereupon these frisky, well-fed Communist leaders of Compound 62 sent word back to their American captors that they intended to fly their Communist flags 'as long and as often as they wanted to'."

This time—one is grateful to learn—the Communists had finally gone too far. When the Swiss delegates received news on February 18th of another eruption of violence at Koje-do, they returned to a scene of utter pandemonium. Compound 62 was out in force, defiantly waving Red flags and chanting Communist battle songs. Reinforced by nearly a regiment of fresh troops, the U. S. Army contingent had thrown a cordon around the enclosure.

From the American camp commander, Colonel Fitzgerald, the Red Cross representatives heard part of the story.

The Colonel had received orders to set up a rescreening of the civilian internees of Compound 62 under conditions which would insure that each prisoner could decide on repatriation without fear of coercion from either Communist or anti-Communist quarters. Discussions with the compound spokesmen having proved completely fruitless, Colonel Fitzgerald summoned additional forces in case of trouble.

U. S. Army troops entered the compound during the night, while most of the prisoners were still asleep; and, by dawn, had split up the large blocks of tents into smaller groups for easy handling. Screening got off to an early start next morning without any difficulties.

But just about the time the camp authorities were ready to congratulate themselves on the smoothness of the whole operation, Compound 76 exploded with a deafening roar. Spearheaded by a well-drilled POW battalion, the Communists advanced to the assault behind tossing Red banners and North Korean flags, armed to the teeth with barbed wire flails, clubs, sharpened tent poles, iron bars, rocks, and homemade Molotov cocktails. Some idea of the savagery of the ensuing clash can be gained from the heavy casualty figures: 79 killed and nearly 150 wounded, among the inmates. One American soldier lost his life and several others were injured.

But the Communists had achieved their purposes: further screening attempts were at a complete standstill.

The scrupulously correct Swiss delegates next interviewed the Communist spokesmen of Compound 62, while they were still exulting in their victory over the American imperialists. Said William L. White:

"According to them, this riot was only a final instance of unprovoked Capitalist aggression against helpless Marxist captives.

"The treachery had begun when the troops had entered the compound 'at 4 in the morning' circling all tents, including that of the head spokesman, who complained he 'had no chance to speak to the camp authorities'.

"As for the Communist attack, the spokesman professed total ignorance as to where that carefully prepared arsenal of homemade weapons had come from. The inmates, who had been ordered to stay in their tents, out of curiosity, merely 'came out to find out what was going on'.

"And if they had advanced on the Americans, this was only in a vain attempt to 'talk to the commander of the troops', not to murder him.

"The Communist spokesman's demands, as transmitted by the Swiss...included (1) that the 79 bodies be returned (for future burial in North Korea), (2) that no more troops come into their compound, and (3) that their report on this be sent to the Secretary General of the United Nations."

A few days later, the Communist spokesmen told the Swiss that they might consider granting permission to the screening teams to enter the compound provided that no UN troops accompanied them. Also, they demanded a halt in the transfer to other compounds of other prisoners who had refused repatriation. This last condition practically amounted to an ultimation; if the camp authorities agreed, it would virtually nullify the whole screening procedure, for the Red leaders would merely continue their reign of terror over dissenting prisoners.

Disturbances, meanwhile, had flared up in other parts of the camp.

On March 13th, some anti-Communist prisoners from Compound 93 were being escorted by ROK soldiers past the barbed wire fence of neighboring Compound 92—a rabidly Communist enclosure. Tempers were high on both sides of the concertina wire, and little provocation was required to trigger off a wild melee. Grabbing the nearest rocks, the Communists launched a barrage of missiles to which the anti-Communists replied with equal vigor. Unluckily for the Reds, however, the ROK guards got caught in the bombardment. Whereupon they opened fire, killing 12 Communist prisoners and wounding 26 others.

The International Red Cross, according to White, now came forward with some carefully considered recommendations:

1 "Withdraw the South Korean guards from Koje-do."
2 "Avoid political demonstrations of any kind, and in particular, the...political program of the Civil Information and Education Service for Prisoners of War." They had once praised our educational program as "excellent," but now politics had become a "constant source of incidents." (Perhaps if the prisoners had neither Communist banners nor American documentary films to inflame them, their political temperatures would fall.)

3 And lastly the Swiss recommended "Distribution of the enormous Koje-do camp amongst smaller camps, which would be more easily controlled."

This was an eminently sensible suggestion, but it was too late by several months. What could have been accomplished without incident at an earlier time henceforth would exact an increasingly stiff price. But it was one that Colonel Fitzgerald would not be called upon to pay. Fitzgerald had been replaced on orders from UN Headquarters in Tokyo by Brigadier General Francis T. Dodd. Thus it was to Colonel Fitzgerald's successor that the Red Cross representative tendered their recommendations.

General Dodd, however, replied that he intended to carry out his orders and go ahead with the rescreening program as planned. Whereupon the Swiss—"officially, ceremoniously, and neutrally"—warned him of the "danger he would be in if force were used."

But the General was presumably to be in more danger than the Swiss, or anyone else for that matter, ever imagined...

CHAPTER FOUR

...And Footfalls Lightly Planted

"The story of the Communist High Command campaign to gain control of the prisoners of war in our compounds and use them as active combatants in our rear is in itself both a case study in the technique of Communist intrigue and a dire warning of the efficiency and imagination of the Communist conspiracy against us."

GENERAL MARK W. CLARK

IN MAY, 1926, a Korean family by the name of Pak—as common in Korea as Smith or Jones in the United States—pulled up stakes and moved to the Soviet Union. Their 12 year-old son, Pak Sang Hyong, dutifully joined the *Komsomol* (Young Communist League); and after completing primary and middle school, enrolled as a student in the college at Khabarovsk, in the Far Eastern provice of Kamchatka. He graduated in 1937, and almost immediately landed a good job as manager of a *kolkhoz*—a collective farm. In 1940, he was admitted to full membership in the Communist Party.

When the war with Japan ended and Russian forces, according to the terms of the Yalta agreement, moved into North Korea, Pak Sang Hyong was working at Tashkent, in Russian Turkestan. Pak was regarded favorably in Party circles, where his diligence, loyalty, and personal qualities had already earmarked him as a man of definite promise. The new situation that was rapidly developing in Korea offered a wider scope for his particular talents. Accordingly, in the casual manner with which such things are handled in a totalitarian state like Soviet Russia, Pak was transferred into the Red Army and shortly found himself wearing a uniform with the shoulder boards of a senior lieutenant. In September, 1945, he was assigned as a staff officer and interpreter to the 25th Red Army Corps in the North Korean capital of Pyongyang. For the next three years, Pak worked closely with the commander, Colonel Kutratchov, of Soviet Army Headquarters.

Since the northern part of Korea had been relegated to Soviet control by Allied agreement, the Communists found it unnecessary to go through the bothersome pretext of wooing the Koreans into willing collaboration. The Russians, who had entered the war against Japan a scant week before her surrender, swarmed into Manchuria and Korea—areas they had long coveted. Their preparations had been thorough: in addition to Soviet-trained Koreans like Pak who entered with the Russian troops, underground Communists suddenly emerged from concealment to take their place alongside newly released Reds who had languished in jail cells for years as political prisoners of the Japanese.

Backed by the armed might of the Red military machine, the Russians—together with their pliant Korean accomplices—proceeded to "democratize" the Koreans north of the 38th parallel in record time. All the familiar apparatus of Communist dictatorship was imported into this small, primitive, remote peninsula.

Pak and his fellow commissars rapidly set up so-called "People's Committees" throughout the country, which the Russians utilized as organs of political control. The propertied class was ruthlessly liquidated—either driven away, permitted to depart empty-handed, tossed into prison, or simply shot. farmers became "tenants of the State" under a sharecropper system which abolished private ownership but retained the worst features of absentee landlordship. So much for "agrarian reform" a la Soviet Russia. Privately owned businesses and factories were also confiscated by the State.

The Russians, through their Korean puppets, ran North Korea as a police state, sealed off from outside intervention by an iron curtain of Soviet tanks and guns. Like the Tartars of old, they lived off the land. Vast quantities of material and equipment, much of it of Japanese origin, left the country bound for Russia. Almost immediately the Communists began assembling and equipping a large army, to which was entrusted the sacred mission of "liberating" the territories to the south from "imperialist" American control.

In February of 1946, representatives of the People's Committees met in Pyongyang to establish a "Democratic People's Republic" for all of Korea. At the head of this government was Kim Il Sung—a Soviet-trained and Soviet-dominated Korean whose name was an alias taken from the well-known patriot and anti-Japanese guerrilla fighter. Kim was another member of that group of Koreans who, like Pak, had returned in the van of the Russian occupation. Under his direction, another Soviet satellite was launched into the Russian political orbit.

The hapless people of North Korea soon discovered that the suppressive features of Japanese domination at its most brutal and terroristic peak were like rampant democracy in comparison with the Communist dictatorship of Kim Il Sung and Company. When United Nations forces thrust into North Korea, they found an impoverished, downtrodden population almost frantically eager for liberation. They found people who were fully prepared to risk death by exposure in the midst of a terrible Korean winter—men, women, and children who fled on foot through the bitterly cold mountains, their few possessions bundled on their heads—rather than face a future of indefinite slavery. It can hardly be denied that Communist attempts to subvert South Korea failed primarily because more than three million North Koreans managed to escape to the south between 1945 and 1950, bringing with them eye-witness accounts of what life was like under Communist tyranny.[1]

In 1950, for the second time in his career, Pak Sang Hyong discovered that war brings challenges and opportunities for an enterprising revolutionary.

A short time earlier, when the Soviet military forces were pulled out of Korea, Pak had received an interesting change in assignments. His new orders directed him to take out citizenship in North Korea and switch his membership from the Russian to the Korean Communist Party. Trading his Red Army uniform for proletarian civvies, he became vice-chairman of the North Korean Labor Party—the softest job he had held thus far. Since all other parties had been abolished in the "Democratic People's Republic," Pak's new position was little more than a sinecure, which left him unencumbered in his real duties as a trusted political *agent provocateur*. It was in this latter capacity that Pak Sang Hyong became one of the UN's most dangerous adversaries.

Late in 1951, United Nations intelligence operatives acquired information that the Communists had organized a special unit charged with the unique task of maintaining combatant status among the prisoners captured by the UNC. Soldiers they had been, and soldiers they were to remain—according to the Communists. This special organization, which was attached to North Korean Army Headquarters, had been given a twofold mission. First, and most important, it was to select and train Communist agents who, having allowed themselves to be captured, would infiltrate UN prisoner of war camps and perform designated leadership tasks. Second, the unit was to set up and monitor an intelligence service to provide information directly to the Communist truce delegation at Panmunjom.

Heading the Red contingent was General Nam Il, a wily, deadpanned, calculating, and resolute Communist officer who had been groomed in the best Russian finishing schools for his role in the takeover of North Korea. Like Kim Il Sung and Pak Sang Hyong, he was a charter member of that original group of 36 Soviet-Koreans brought in by the Russians in 1945 to Communize North Korea. At the time he was directing cease-fire negotiations at Panmunjom, Nam Il was still at the controls of the most high-powered machinery in the North Korean Army—the so-called "Political Control Organization." "This was the familiar Communist commissar system," noted General Mark Clark. "In Korea it had the broadest kind of powers. It did everything from dealing out physical punishment to traitors to censoring mail of North Korean foot soldiers. It published newspapers, organized service shows, handled troop indoctrination, spied for dissident elements in the army, trained and assigned agents and controlled a soldier's career by either admitting him to or suspending him from party membership."

To this already powerful organization was entrusted the additional task of inciting disturbances within the United Nations POW camps.

The first evidence the UNC received of successful *organized* Communist infiltration of the prison compounds came in December of 1951, when UN intelligence agents intercepted a message bearing the signature of the head of the Southern Section of the Communist Korean Labor Party. This document reported that, "According to information from the party in Kyongsang Namdo, South Korea, approximately thirty thousand to sixty thousand North Korean Army soldiers interned in the Koje-do prisoner-of-war camp have been organized and the Kyongsang Namdo Branch of the Korean Labor Communist Party will start activities in their behalf."

Intelligence interrogation subsequently revealed that many POW's were deliberate plants—Communist agents who had allowed themselves to be captured so that they could carry messages, orders, and plans into the UN camps. Said General Clark:

> "Male agents were dispersed in front-line Communist units and, during small skirmishes with UN troops, either surrendered or were 'captured.' They then were put into the normal UN prisoner-of-war channels and transported to their goal by us, undetected. Women agents were sent south as refugees with instructions to find work in or near POW hospitals or camps so they could help the Red agents inside the barbed wire compounds.
>
> "The men and women picked for these jobs as agents in and around the POW Camps were Communist Party members of good standing who had demonstrated that they were hard-core Communists. After they were picked for the job they were given an intensive two-month training course in the history of the USSR Communist Party and the Korean Labor Party, Communist theory,methods of organizing military and civilian party groups, Korean revolution and the world situation and the situation in South Korea. The agents were directed specifically to spread propaganda among the prisoners to the effect that unification of Korea under the North Korean Government was a certainty and that withdrawal of United Nations forces from Korea was imminent.
>
> "The agents also were instructed to emphasize to the POW's that modern equipment was being given to the North Korean Army by the Soviet Union and China, that the life of the North Korean soldier had vastly improved, that high North Korean Government

officials were concerned about the welfare of the prisoners of war and that high respect and consideration would be shown them when they returned."

Communist agents themselves were not exempted from "brain washing" by their own leaders. Intensive Red indoctrination had succeeded to the extent that many Communist soldiers were convinced the UN Command had a standard policy of shooting prisoners. Communist bosses were obliged to take measures to counteract the effects of their mendacious propaganda: agents about to surrender or let themselves be captured were told that the prospects of an armistice had put an end to these murderous United Nations practices. Furthermore, the Communist operatives were promised a hero's welcome from the North Korean people when they returned from their mission. To make their assertions even more convincing, the Communist leaders suggested that, in view of the imminence of a cease-fire agreement, the term of voluntary captivity would be bearably short.

"The assigned missions," General Clark stated, "followed a definite pattern and plan. Each agent was instructed to establish 'cell organization committees' in each POW camp, North Korean officers were to be assigned by the agents to responsible positions within the network of Red cells so they could enforce rigid military discipline. As the cells grew strong and their control of the prison compounds became trustworthy, they were to instigate and carry out strikes, protests and demonstrations."

In addition, the agent's functions included maintaining a close check on the attitudes and activities of each prisoner. "The specific instructions directed the agent to obtain the names of those who had deserted or surrendered voluntarily, those who were unsympathetic to the North Korean Government and those who were suspected informers because of the frequency with which they were questioned by

Allied camp authorities. In addition the agents were to get the names of the Republic of Korea guards and all informers posing as prisoners. These names were to be used for future reference, when the Communists were able to prosecute 'war criminals' in Korea."

High on the list of assigned priorities was the establishment of an effective communications system. Several considerations were involved: the means for transmitting orders and information from one compound to another within the camp itself, provisions for smuggling messages back to the Communist authorities in North Korea, and—most important—setting up communication links between the agents in the camp and the Communist High Command. By the time the Dodd incident occurred, all of these aims had been met. The Communists had fashioned a tightly-knit, cohesive, and smoothly functioning organization, both within as well as outside the camp.

Clearing center for the exchange of messages between compounds was the U. S. Army 64th Field Hospital, which furnished medical care for the POW's. Feigning illness, a prisoner with information to forward gained admittance to the hospital, where his message would then be transmitted verbally or by means of a note tied to a rock and tossed from one compound to the next until it reached its destination.

Operations were directed and coordinated within the officers' ward—nerve center of the hospital communications network. Everything that passed through the system—orders, information, directives—came under the scrutiny of the Communist leaders in this ward. From there the material was disseminated among the various compounds by patients released from the hospital upon the conclusion of their 'treatment.'

The system should have been familiar to the Koje camp authorities, for it is the same procedure used by Allied POW's during World War II in German stalags and by inmates of our own penal institutions in the United States. But the Communists added one or two wrinkles of their own. Strict military organization, for example, was maintained within the hospital. Each ward was designated as a *yuk* (company), and a group of wards comprised a *ku* (battalion). Reliable prisoners were assigned positions of military command and ran the wards exactly like military units.

Prisoners working at various "trustee" jobs in the hospital were either press-ganged into cooperation with the Communists or else joined them voluntarily. Ward leaders grilled each prisoner to determine the hue of his political complexion. If the prisoner passed this Communist screening, he was absorbed into the Korean Labor Party as an active member and fitted into the communications organization.

"Good military practice in any army," General Clark observed, "dictates that a commander must provide alternate means of communication. The Communist prisoners on Koje were no exception. Although the hospital was the best channel for intercompound commucations, there were alternate methods, including semaphore flags, hand signals, whistling, chanting and throwing messages tied to rocks. Messages also were hidden in rations, clothing and supplies being delivered to the compounds. No possible means of communication was overlooked, as evidenced by the effort of some prisoners to tie messages to large dragonflies."

To augment this Koje Island communications set-up and insure effective coordination between the Communist POW's and the armistice negotiators at Panmunjom, the Communist High Command made use of two additional agencies: the Guerrilla Guidance Bureau and the Espionage Department—an elite corps— of the North Korean Army Military Intelligence Section.

General Pae Chol, still another Soviet-trained Korean officer, headed the Guerrilla Guidance Bureau. This organization supplied the couriers who carried messages from the POW's to the Communist High Command.

The functions of the Guidance Bureau were supplemented by ten- or twelve-man intelligence teams provided by the Espionage Department. Teams were commanded by officers ranging in rank from senior lieutenant to full colonel, and normally included a few seasoned NCO's. Each team was equipped with a portable radio of Russian make, on which messages could be received but not transmitted. The Espionage Department also operated an extensive spy network in South Korea. According to Mark Clark:

> "Allied authorities confiscated many messages from prisoners inside the compounds, including some addressed to Mao Tse-tung in Peiping and Kim Il Sung in Pyongyang.
>
> "The method of passing messages in and out of the compounds was so simple as to be elementary. There were many civilians on the island, including a village in the general area of the prison camp. Agents lived in the village and mingled with the people. These agents dropped notes where prisoner work detail members could find them. Members of the work details got word out of the compounds and into the Communist communications network by the same method, dropping notes where agents could pick them up.
>
> "Effective liaison with the North Korean Army Headquarters was made possible by the tight political and then military organization of the Communists inside the compounds. It was the political organization which developed a section to make contact with Communists outside the compounds so that the note-drop grapevine could be established."

And this political organization—which went by the innocent sounding title "General Leading Headquarters"—was headed by an old, trustworthy, familiar Communist boss.

Listed among the names on the United Nations Command roster of POW's was that of "Jeon Moon Il," private in the North Korean Army. Despite the comparative squalor of his rank, Private Jeon seemed to wield a disproportionately powerful influence over the other prisoners in the camp. Even within Compound 66, which housed North Korean officers, prisoners like Colonel Lee deferred to Private Jeon's authority. It was to this lowly private that newly arrived Red agents first reported. It was Private Jeon who issued orders, initiated directives, and planned propaganda. And it was Jeon who passed the death sentence on prisoners who had dared to show defiance toward the Communist Party.

Private Jeon Moon Il, of course, was none other than Pak Sang Hyong. He had allowed himself to be captured and sent to Koje-do, where, as top-ranking political officer, he assumed control of the Communist POW organization.

Intensive Red political agitation had started at Koje-do back in the spring of 1951. By the end of May, the Communists had organized the first cells in Compound 62. Identical branches of the Korean Communist Labor Party were soon founded in other compounds. The following general statement of Communist aims and principles was circulated freely among these political groups:

"We are reborn members of the Party and will sacrifice our lives and display all our ability for the Party so that the North Korean People's Republic may win the final victory.

"We are reborn members of the Party and will be faithful to the Party and carry out the Party's proclamation to educate all prisoners of war.

"Our Party will implement the platform of the People's Republic to have all prisoners of war, indigenous refugees, or officers and soldiers of the Republic of Korea recognize the platform.

"Our Party will foster internationalism, try to be friendly with the Chinese Communist forces, and infuse class consciousness into United Nations soldiers."

With the development of an efficient communications system, the instructions and orders that poured into Koje-do through the pipeline from Panmunjom became increasingly bold in aim and detailed in direction:

"We must consider the possible rupture of the cease-fire negotiations which are now underway (said one declaration of objectives) and be ready to liberate ourselves in accordance with orders from Kim Il Sung. The prisoners of war should educate themselves and surround themselves with Party members. All types of units must be organized to rise in revolt simultaneously in order to liberate all the prisoners of war and attack the ROK (Republic of Korea) and American forces that now occupy Koje-do. After we win autonomous rights we will keep in touch with the commanding officer of the North Korean People's Army by wireless and will land on Korea proper. After that we will join the NKPA(North Korean People's Army) together with the Chiri-san guerrilla units."[2]

At Nam Il's direction, a political committee was established in the Koje camp to consolidate Communist control. The four sections of this "General Leading Headquarters"—Political Security, Organization and Planning, Guard Unit, and Agitprop—had specifically detailed functions and responsibilities. According to General Clark's account:

"The First Section, Political Security, policed Party members to eliminate those guilty of 'factionalism, opportunism and cowardice', to select 'superior experienced members' for key jobs, to recruit Party members and to 'take precautionary measures against spies and agents to include agents of the Republic of Korea Army, civil interpreters, Christian ministers, Party members with bad qualities, religionists, former security chiefs, draft evaders, reactionary groups and those who associate with reactionary elements'. All these were to be 'blacklisted'. The First Section placed trusted Communists in each company, platoon and squad. The agents kept their affiliation secret so they could spy on their fellows in the military-type units."

Section Number Two—Organization and Planning—handled the preparation of intelligence reports on camp guards, collected and distributed news, and maintained liaison with guerrilla forces outside the camp which transmitted messages between the POW compounds and the Communist High Command. The subsection for "External Liaison and Reconnaissance" received explicit and detailed orders for establishing contact with Red partisans on the Korean mainland in anticipation of any mass break-outs. One directive to this subordinate command read in part as follows:

"Whenever the time is appropriate for an uprising or break, the members dispatched to the outside will assist the basic fighting units to get out of the compound by occupying stationary firing posts and guard posts by surprise attack, light signal fires on the hills, capture weapons and destroy United Nations ammunition and armory store houses. This subsection will be organized from Party members experienced in guerrilla fighting in China and South Korea, those who have a thorough knowledge of enemy weapons and those who served in the North Korean Army in engineering and reconnaissance."

Escapees also received instructions on definite procedures to be followed once they had got free of the camp area:

"After extrication (the instructions said) construct a partisan base and set fire to the camp's headquarters petroleum dump, food storage and other supply areas and destroy the transportation route. After completion of this duty, they will get to the mainland and report to an officer higher than major and join the partisans. Extrication or escape will be accomplished before dawn, while on work details or during foggy weather."

Another subsection of Organization and Planning, designated as "External Intelligence," carried out the task of collecting "straight military intelligence on all Allied units and movements on the island, plus the nonmilitary task of compiling the full name, age, birthplace, address and political ideas of all ROK soldiers, police, civilians and government officials."

The third section, or "Guard Unit," included one subdivision which was charged with safeguarding the security of General Leading Headquarters staff members. Said Clark:

"The Guard Unit not only had to protect staff members from attack, but was even admonished that 'constant care should be exercised regarding the staff's health conditions (securing their health, food and clothes)'. That adds up to a system in which the Communist bosses had prisoners assigned to them as orderlies."

Another group in the Guard Unit functioned as an execution squad. This detachment was directed to "punish, beat and execute violators condemned by the 'people's courts'"—a Communist euphemism for Kangaroo courts. "There was ample work for the executioners," General Clark observed, "for the People's Courts were busy. Intelligence files of the United Nations Command are filled with accounts of executions in the compounds." The methods used by the Red bosses to bulldoze prisoners into obedience are illustrated by the following report:

"A 1,000-man 'jury' (250 men from each battalion) on June 6, 1952, conducted a 'self criticism' of prisoners and sentenced one to death. The prisoner who received the death sentence was a member of an anti-communist group, which, it was alleged, had plotted to kill the communist leaders and take control of Compound 85.

"In December, 1951, three prisoners were stoned to death on orders of the communist 'people's court'.

"A prisoner accused of being anti-communist refused to speak before the Chief of the Political Committee in compound 66 on November 11, 1951. All platoon members kicked or struck the prisoner. Two of them then took a section of a tent pole and beat him to death."

Assassination was not outside the scope of their activities, as shown by the events that transpired in Compound 65—the only enclosure on Koje-do, according to Colonel Hansen, which never fell under the control of the Communists at any time:

"After an abortive attempt to seize control of the compound on May 20 (1951) the Communists instigated a fullscale riot on the 16th of August. Two thousand additional POWs had been added to the compound, for a total of 10,000, and to preserve internal order among so many men 105 'compound monitors' had been elected. The compound monitors put down the riot without having to call on the UNC authorities for assistance, and arrested and turned over to the camp command the 22 Communist ringleaders. A flare-up of rioting at reveille the next morning was also suppressed, and 78 additional Communists arrested. The compound monitor intelligence system, getting wind of a planned third riot, twice intercepted orders for it, again arrested the ringleaders, and prevented it completely...

"Having failed to secure control of the compound by force, the diminished Communist element turned to a standard Red device—assassination—with Lee Dong Je and Lee Sung Baek (the duly elected compound leader and his predecessor) as their principal targets. Communist agent Lyu In Soon pretended illness and was admitted to the headquarters hospital. There, fellow agent Kim Hong Tae passed him a small quantity of poison which he had procured from a North Korean Communist medical officer on duty in the hospital. A third agent, Han Man Sik, who was a member of the kitchen police, was to put this poison in the leaders' soup as he served the evening meal.

"But surveillance by the compound monitors of the security of the leaders was so strict that Han had no opportunity to poison the soup unobserved. He buried the poison near the latrine—and was caught in the act. That was the last gasp of Communism in Compound 65."

It was far from the last gasp, however, in other compounds at Koje.

Agitprop—the fourth section dealing with political agitation and propaganda—was one of the busiest subcommittees of General Leading Headquarters. The members of this section drafted plans and programs of indoctrination and propaganda and also maintained documents and statistics.

"Once the political apparatus was organized," said General Clark, "Military Administrative Committees were created in various compounds. The committees established brigade or regimental headquarters to which the compound spokesman, interpreter, monitor and security chief were attached. The battalion, immediately below brigade or regiment, was the basic 'fighting' unit and was broken down, in good military order, into three or four companies, each of which was divided into platoons and squads."

Pak Sang Hyong later boasted to UN intelligence operatives: "I had a whole division under my command. We could easily have taken Koje, but how could we have left the island?"

In April of 1952, Pak received new and urgent orders from Nam Il. Not only were the Red POW's to resist to the death any attempts at screening and segregation of anti-Communists in the compounds they controlled, but they were also to seize an American officer—preferably of high rank—and, using his life as a bargaining factor, extract from the UN Command a guarantee to drop any further screening operations.

With these orders from Panmunjom, Pak issued new instructions to the POW colonels, captains and sergeants in all Communist-dominated compounds:

> "In the event of entry by UN troops, 1,500 Communist prisoners will lead the attack and be led by the compound commandant and vice-commandant. This first line will be backed by 3,500 other prisoners led by their platoon leaders. The estimated 2,500 anti-Communist prisoners will remain in their quarters and not join in the attack. The plan is to attack UN troops from the flanks, capturing weapons and troops, preferably officers. The weapons to be utilized in the attack are spears made from tent poles, a piece of pipe six inches long, knives, flails and clubs."

Pak's organization had already planned and executed several minor disturbances. Discipline among the Reds was razor-sharp; "deviationists" and backsliders were punished without mercy. But these sporadic outbursts of violence were merely preliminaries.

The real Communist reign of terror was about to begin in earnest...

CHAPTER FIVE

Brainwashing–U.S. Style

"PSYCHOLOGICAL WARFARE", a well-known expert in the field once observed, is "planned along the edge of nightmare." For fighting men of the United Nations who were taken prisoner by the Communists during the Korean conflict, Paul Linebarger's dramatic characterization can be spelled out in a hundred, a thousand, horribly literal examples—each one a page torn from the calendar of their captivity. Using an approach that has since been identified as "brainwashing"—an expression translated from the Chinese *hsi nau*, which stands for a combination of old and new procedures in indoctrination—the Communists transferred their assault against the free world from the battlefront to the POW camp. There they sought to achieve the victories they had been denied in battle. Historians may someday record that the real war in Korea was the one fought behind barbed wire for the minds of men from both sides.

In this kind of struggle, terms like victory and defeat acquire new dimensions of meaning. Progress is measured by subtle standards: minute but perceptible changes in values, shifts of allegiance, alterations in social norms and codes of conduct. Old symbols break down and are replaced with others that suddenly take on special significance.

Many excellent and authoritative accounts have been written about Communist brainwashing and its successful use in the infamous Red prison camps on captured United Nations personnel—the 21 American GI defectors, the "progressives" who collaborated with the enemy for personal advantage, the germ-warfare confessions that were extracted from our captive airmen, and so on. Surprisingly little has been written about the results of our own "Made in U.S.A." brand of indoctrination among the Communist prisoners of war at Koje-do and elsewhere. The average American citizen would probably be astonished to learn that, in comparison with what the Reds achieved in their POW camps, the United Nations Command program of education in democracy proved an overwhelming victory for the free world. As Colonel Hansen said, "When one considers the total numbers of Koreans, Americans and Britons who fell into Communist hands in the Korean conflict, the number of non-repatriates is a testimonial not to the efficacy but to the almost total failure of brainwashing. When one considers in addition the complete total of 88,000 Koreans and Chinese who chose freedom at the first opportunity after escaping from Communist control, it is small wonder that the tune from the Kremlin, between conditioned-reflex blasts of belligerence, periodically harps on peaceful coexistence." In sheer numbers alone, therefore, the relative success of our "brainwashing" efforts reduces to insignificance the Red achievements, and constitutes one of the few glittering accomplishments in a wasteland strewn with failures.

In the fall of 1950, the military situation in Korea had been altered overnight by a single decisive stroke: MacArthur's audaciously conceived and flawlessly executed "end run" at Inchon. During the weeks of precipitate retreat that followed this successful amphibious operation, the North Korean "People's Army" practically ceased to exist as a fighting force. As the United Nations Command pursued the rapidly disintegrating Communist armies up the Korean peninsula, it soon found itself encumbered with masses of captured Red soldiers. Over 60,000 prisoners fell into our hands in a matter of only a few weeks. A minority of these were bitter, doctrinaire Communists with a venomous hatred for anything American who proved definitely more troublesome as POW's than they had as soldiers. A larger number of captives, however, apparently had been press-ganged into uniform by the Reds. Simple farmers for the most part, they were almost docile enough to be sent to the rear unescorted.

With many, opposition toward the Communists went even further. A surprising number of POW's startled their captors by asking how soon they could expect to be outfitted and rearmed—so that they could join the United Nations forces in the fight against Communism!

Old Asia hands on the UNC staff were quick to point out that "turning around" prisoners (i.e., arming them to fight their former rulers) was in the best Oriental traditions—a custom the Chinese warlords had practiced for centuries. Nevertheless, the enthusiasm with which these men volunteered to serve against their late Communist overseers was unmistakable. Perhaps more was involved here than mere deference to established custom.

The Geneva Convention—which the Communists generally ignored and to which at all times we scrupulously adhered—expressly forbids such practices. But there is nothing in the Convention which denies a prisoner of war the right to an education, provided no compulsion is brought to bear by the detaining power. Communism, it was decided in Washington, can be combatted just as effectively on this front as on the battlefield.

From this germ of an idea sprouted "Rehabilitation Project for Prisoners of War," a program which received the personal indorsement of President Truman. With singular good fortune, the U.S. Army obtained the services of a remarkable man, Mr. Monta L.

Osborne, as head of the educational part of the project. A former major in the Army, Osborne had spent more than a decade in the Far East and had worked closely with the Chinese government during World War II. After the war, as a civilian employee of the Army, he had been in charge of selecting democratic textbooks for Japanese schoolchildren under the Occupation. His job had recently come to an end with the restoration of sovereignty to Japan.

The pilot project he headed got off to a rather modest start. As William L. White described it:

> "Under Osborne the Army took 500 POW's chosen as a cross section in age, education, politics, and occupation. Most were simple farmers. Then, in dwindling percentages, they were laborers, clerks, merchants, and teachers. This test-tube sample was assembled near Seoul at Yongdungpo.
>
> "Why were they there? Osborne told these 500 guinea-pig POW's that his hope was to show them the Free World's viewpoint, which they had never experienced because previously they had only known the thought control of Imperial Japan, followed, in 1945, by that of the Soviet Union.
>
> "If what they were told puzzled or annoyed them, they were free to put questions or to protest. If they disliked any or all of his educational program, they were free to stay away entirely.
>
> "Propaganda cafeteria style?—not even that. For Osborne's program contained no sneers at Stalin or scowls at North Korean Communism—aimed only to show the ways and viewpoint of the Free World."

U.S. Information Service came to the aid of the project. A weekly translation of the USIS news releases was provided for the prisoners, as well as copies of the magazine *America*. The ROK government also cooperated in the rehabilitation program by making various prominent South Koreans—educators, businessmen, diplomats, and government officials—available as lecturers. Many distinguished VIP's travelled to Yongdungpo to explain to the prisoners what steps were being taken to establish the Republic of Korea as a stable, efficient representative democracy. "Their talks," said Colonel Hansen, "as well as the pamphlets distributed to the 500, were used as a basis for group discussions, and the avidity with which the men seized on the first opportunity in their lives for self-expression was remarkable. Their whole-hearted participation in the project did not stop with the formal sessions. The more literate were observed, during the first week-end they were gathered together, reading the pamphlets to the less well educated and then discussing them."

Newsreels that had been prepared by USIS for use in explaining the ways of democracy to the Japanese were also turned over to the pilot project—with consequences of both an amusing and an instructive nature. Thirty-five years of Japanese domination had made the average Korean bilingual. However, since many Koreans still harbor strong feelings of resentment toward their former Japanese overlords, Osborne decided to show the films with the Japanese language sound tracks disconnected.

"Then one day," said White, "a projectionist fumbled, and the prisoners discovered that those silent movies had Japanese sound. Why could they not hear it? Osborne answered that we had cut it, lest some be offended. Would they like to vote on this? More than 95% balloted yes. Now Osborne gave them their second lesson in Democracy, which was that the 5% minority which disliked Japanese also had its rights. So they said, run it again for these with no sound track, but with explainers speaking Korean."

After only one week, 20 prisoners—representing a variety of occupational and educational backgrounds—were selected to lead a discussion forum. They were given an opportunity to explain, in three-minute talks to the assembled 500 prisoners, "My Part in This War." Their talks covered the circumstances under which they had been taken into the North Korean People's Army, what the Communist authorities had told them about their war objectives, and what was their own outlook on the subject at the present time.

"Although these speakers were really volunteers," Colonel Hansen noted, "they were, for the most part, exceedingly shy, afraid of the microphone and acutely embarrassed. But when they heard their voices coming back over the loudspeakers, they gained courage, and after the first seminar the problem was not in obtaining volunteers but in picking twenty men from five hundred volunteers."

These prisoners were men of real courage; for at this particular time, there was absolutely no basis for assuming that any of the POW's would be exempted from forcible repatriation. They were bitterly critical nonetheless of the Communist regime.

One of the first speakers opened with a grateful testimonial to Mr. Osborne and his staff:

> "First of all, I must express my gratitude at this opportunity. You, chief educator and other instructors, are so kind and good as to give us, the very captives, many books and newspapers in behalf of our education, and to permit us to explain our opinions freely. This kind of thing we could hardly dream of even a few days ago. We are now very much delighted and hopeful.
>
> "On June 25th 1950 we were driven down by the puppet leadership from North Korea with the object of the so-called liberation of our fatherland. The communist leaders always advocated that only we, the North Koreans, were on the side of justice, and, therefore, had the righteous urge to liberate Southern Korea at the risk of our lives. We were thus misled by such propaganda, and in sheer igno-

rance of truth. But now we view the matter in its true light."
Another speaker said:

"We are already convinced that we were misled and deceived by the communist party. Now that we know, why can't we join the ROK Army now, instead of spending a few months in this camp? I have talked to many, and many of us want to join the ROK Army."

Those "few months" of captivity, unfortunately, were destined to stretch into more than three years. Before these prisoners were given an opportunity to join the United Nations forces in the common struggle against Communist tyranny, they were compelled to suffer Communist depredations within the prison compounds of Koje-do. Their loyalties were subjected to the most rigorous trials one can imagine. Yet their resolute spirit remained undaunted, and their numbers grew from a few hundred to many thousands:

Communist ruthlessness, Colonel Hansen pointed out, was born out in shocking detail in their personal histories:

"One 18 year old, a middle school graduate employed in a factory, said that just one month before the invasion of South Korea, 'inspectors' came to the factory to persuade him to 'enlist' in the army. When he still demurred after several visits, he was informed that he would be discharged from the factory and deprived of his rations. He 'enlisted,' and with no military training whatever participated in the June 25th attack."

"A miner and a student similarly demurred until they were thrown into jail. Seven other students, finding that graduation day in early June was conscription day, fled their homes, only to be pursued by the police and caught. Two other students were given no opportunity to flee. A carpenter who was the sole support of his mother fled unsuccessfully; the police simply jailed his mother, and he returned to secure her release. One farmer, with several friends from his village, hid out in the mountains for 25 days, but they all came back, too, when they heard what was happening to their families. Three brothers, farmers, fled just before their harvest, but came back in two weeks for the same reason. Few had had more than a day or two of military training. None wanted to return to such a system—and small wonder."

Monta Osborne's experiment was barely a month old, when the Korean war went into extra innings. The entrance of the Red Chinese "volunteers" made it a brand new ball-game. To escape being drowned in the human flood[1] that poured down from the icy wastes of Manchuria in December of 1950, the UN Command broke up the pilot project and moved Osborne's 500 experimental subjects to Pusan, along with thousands of other prisoners.

Most of these 500 eagerly sought to enlist in the ROK Army—despite the fact that the South Korean forces were in full retreat. They were quite put out when the UN authorities informed them that their part in the war was over—that they would have to sweat out the duration behind barbed wire.

"As we swept the fragments of this little experiment into our huge prison camps to the south," said William L. White, "we had no idea that anything further would come of it. We had learned what we wanted to know which was that North Koreans, once exposed to concepts of freedom and fair play, would just as eagerly grasp them as had those of the South. Like other pieces of seemingly useless information, the results of 'Rehabilitation Project: POW' were shelved and for a time forgotten. It was, however, curious that so few of those 500 had wanted to return to North Korea. That we remembered."

After that dark December of 1950, affairs took an upswing for the United Nations Command. The panicky retreat which witnessed a triumphant Communist reoccupation of Seoul—this time by Chinese "volunteers," along with the rejuvenated North Korean Army—ended about 25 or 30 miles south of the Han River instead of on the outskirts of Pusan. There the UN forces rallied and beat off several determined Red thrusts. Then they went over to the offensive themselves. By April of 1951, they had thrown the Communists out of Seoul for the second time.

April had brought another crisis: the relief from command of General Douglas MacArthur. Thus a resolution of sorts had been made in the long wrangle between the authorities in Washington and the military commander on the spot—a recurring theme in American civil-military relations. Partisan supporters of MacArthur and Truman, respectively, showed a readiness to debate the pros and cons of the matter with brickbats, as well as words. At any rate, one of the most colorful and controversial figures who ever wore the uniform of the U.S. Army turned over his command to General Matthew B. Ridgway with a minimum of fuss and fanfare, and departed for the United States where a hero's welcome awaited him.

But one of MacArthur's last orders still held. Remembering the success of the pilot project in POW rehabilitation, MacArthur recommended it for more general application in the compounds at Koje Island. "While the POW's were being moved from Seoul and Inchon to Pusan and Koje-do," Hansen noted, "plans went forward swiftly for resumption of the rehabilitation program as soon as they were settled. Not for just five hundred men this time, but for all of the thousands of North Koreans in hand, the Chinese who were beginning to accumulate behind barbed wire, and thousands who were still to come."

By an odd coincidence, April was the same month the Communists chose to initiate their own indoctrination program among UN captives in the prison camps near the Yalu River.

For the upwards of 100,000 prisoners we held at that time, winter had passed with a minimum of discomfort. The average Korean and Chinese captive had gained two pounds per month on UN rations and the death rate among the prisoners compared favorably with the disease rate among our own troops. In fact, it was even lower, for illnesses like the dreaded hemorrhagic fever—which took a cruel toll of American lives during the Korean conflict—are endemic among the Korean people.

We had also paid scrupulous attention to Article 26 in the Geneva Convention, which specifies that "account shall be taken of the habitual diet of prisoners." Culinary experts in the Pentagon had labored overtime to reconcile any differences between the habitual diet of the prisoners of war and that of our own troops. Said William L. White:

"Just as certain Oriental delicacies such as fragrant stewed dog, pickled seaweed, and octopus tenderly simmered in its own ink lack for Western appetites an instant appeal, so Orientals fail to warm up to some of our strange Western dainties. Instead the prisoners got what they wanted, bolstered by plenty of rice, and in late winter all were busy planting spring gardens, which would produce an abundance of tomatoes, potatoes, Chinese cabbage, and cauliflower.

"Scan now the official report of neutral Swiss IRC Delegate, Frederick Bieri, who in late November dropped in on our POW Camp 1 at Pusan. Here he found 91,662 POW's getting '3 meals daily' and that '69 tons of rice and barley are now transported daily to the camps'. He found that 'large amounts of winter clothing have already reached Korea' so that, 'in Pusan, every POW has received either greatcoats, jackets or else warm underwear; many have both'.

"Under 'Medical Care' he reports 'nutrition: poor on arrival, good after 10–14 days'. Of more than 3,000 patients in the POW hospital, since September 9th only 226 had died '—of these, most died on arrival'.

"Under 'Complaints: none. The POW seem content with their lot. The finest feature is the first class medical care, which is very much appreciated by the POW. The camp commanders are all the right men in the right places, who do what they can for their charges...an excellent camp.' So for the moment we leave them, but with this final word: that later when this pastoral idyll was to change, and bloody civil war break out among these prisoners, there was not to be the slightest difference between the food we provided in Communist and anti-Communist compounds. The Communists who were to stone our soldiers and kidnap our unwary generals fought us on plump bellies, and smoking their daily share of our American cigarettes."

Although we had already made a shift to separate the prisoners according to a rough division between Communist and anti-Communist affiliations, no real concern was shown at this point for the further consequences of this internecine political strife. Our tolerant, easygoing, indulgent attitude helped considerably to smooth the path for the Communists' accession to power.

When he visited Koje Island in the spring of 1952, O.H.P. King—author of *Tail of the Paper Tiger*—found the expanded POW rehabilitation project in full swing. "In addition to intensive reading, writing, and arithmetic instruction to wipe out illiteracy," he wrote, "there were book courses in government, education, and history, but by far the most popular were the mechanical arts. The various crafts, woodshop, machineshop, and other useful activities of which the average POW had no knowledge at all, were taught, that Korea would be enriched by the prisoners' skills and that they would be better able to cope with the problem of earning a living in an awakened hermit kingdom.

"Prisoners became able machinists. They learned to use forges and make objects of iron and steel. When I asked in amazement if it was not dangerous for prisoners to be provided with the means of manufacturing weapons, I was assured that a close watch was kept on all materials brought into the shops, but the value of the training given the men was much greater than the danger, and the good morale engendered by the free instruction was a significant factor in maintaining order.

"Indoctrination? Yes, there were education courses that could have been described by unfriendly critics as designed to reeducate the Communists, to acquaint them with democratic theories and practices, to teach them that the state existed to serve the individual, not the reverse, but these courses were not compulsory and no penalty or other discrimination was imposed upon those not attending. The general thirst for knowledge was great, it was explained, and most men preferred to improve themselves through regular use of both the mental and physical facilities offered rather than to sit around in idleness."

The thirst for knowledge of which King speaks was clearly demonstrated in the earlier pilot project. Communist suppression of news had only served to create an insatiable curiosity among the North Korean and Chinese people about the rest of the world—particularly the free world—and the activities of people of other countries. The UN staff tried to satisfy this curiosity by offering classes in current events. Said Colonel Hansen:

> "Attendance at these classes too was voluntary. In anti-Communist compounds they were crowded. In compounds in which the ideological struggle had not yet been resolved, attendance was limited to anti-Communists and Communist leaders, the latter picking

up names of articulate anti-Communists for later liquidation, and arguments for use in the inevitable brainwashing sessions to follow. After the screenings and clear-cut separation of Communist and anti-Communist compounds in 1952, the orientation classes were dropped entirely as far as the Communists were concerned.

"Orientation was a better name for these classes than current events, particularly for the North Koreans, who had to be updated to the twentieth century historically before any attempt could be made to brief them on the problems of Korea as it entered the second half of that century. Men of military age, their concepts had been formed under an increasing barrage of Japanese propaganda culminating in an almost complete absence of information during War II. Then, suddenly, they had become targets of the usual flood of Communist misinformation.

"None of them had any inkling of the post-war attempts of the United Nations to unify Korea, and the fact that these attempts had been thwarted by Soviet Russia. All of the officers knew that North Korea had invaded the Republic of Korea at Soviet instigation, but many of the common soldiers quite genuinely believed that their thrust into South Korea had been made in repelling an attack upon North Korea by the 'American imperialists'."

Among the Chinese prisoners, the level of sophistication was considerably higher. They had not suffered, like the North Koreans, nearly two generations of political isolation and foreign domination. But their knowledge of recent events was equally sketchy. UN interrogators could obtain a fairly accurate fix on the date their village or province had been Communized by simply asking them to recall the last time they had read a non-Communist newspaper or listened to a non-Communist radio broadcast.

"To have compelled these men to attend these classes would have been futile," Colonel Hansen asserted, "and nothing whatever would have been accomplished. The time they had spent in interminable Communist classes, forced to listen, to confess, to parrot in chorus, had rendered them almost immune to indoctrination. But the orientation classes were voluntary. They were interesting and informative, and the eagerness of these men to learn was pathetic. The Communist version of recent history was noted, and the free world version presented. The instructors gave them the facts, and left it up to them to make up their own minds. There were among them sufficient officers and natural leaders who knew the Communist versions to be false, and their own shrewdness had often told them that Communist insistence on certain points pointed to their untruth. In their own discussions they arrived at sound conclusions quite penetratingly."

Progress was rapid. Using a whole arsenal of training aids and teaching techniques which the Army language training program has employed with remarkable success in turning out skilled linguists in less than eighteen months, the Koje instructional staff crammed months of education into weeks. The emphasis was on visual aids and group discussion; lectures and explanations were held to a minimum and kept as brief as possible. Programs were limited only by the scarcity of materials and the ingenuity of the teachers and POW students. Said Hansen:

> "When a subject would lend itself to dramatization, skits and playlets or puppet shows were presented, by the instructors, instructors and students, or the students themselves.
>
> "Exhibits and poster displays were contrived in conjunction with instruction, and then left as semi-permanent displays in the instruction centers, where the men could inspect and discuss them at their leisure. Panel discussions, forums, symposiums and similar methods

were employed to tie the students in with the instruction and stimulate them to positive thinking.

"Radio broadcasts were simulated, and the Chinese prisoners of war took to the microphone even more readily than the Koreans in the pilot project. Quiz shows, general discussions, question and answer periods and speeches and dialogues by students were employed. Compositions and themes written by the prisoners of war were read and discussed in class meetings, and talks and oral reports by the students were regular features. Recorded radio programs were played, and followed by discussion."

Perhaps one anecdote will serve to demonstrate the thoroughness with which the prisoner of war students identified with the rehabilitation project and the pride they took in its accomplishments. At the anti-Communist Camp 9 in Pusan, the prisoner-constructed building which was used as both a classroom and a theater suddenly sported gleaming white walls in the dressing rooms. Camp authorities were completely mystified: to the best of their knowledge, not a single bucket of whitewash was to be had in Korea. But the mystery was shortly solved when they discovered that the whitewash was another example of Korean ingenuity.

To make it, the prisoners had donated their entire three months' supply of tooth powder.

Support for the rehabilitation project was often lacking in the early days from the camp commanders. "Driven first to get the camps of Koje built to house the prisoners, then getting the hutments winterized, they were impatient with anything which might interfere with work details," said Colonel Hansen. "It was difficult for them to see any sense in teaching arithmetic to an adult Korean or calligraphy to a Chinese... They rebelled even more when the vocational training program got under way, until they discovered that this could help them accomplish their own missions. The POW camps were at the end of the supply lines in Korea. There was the usual argument there between the combat troops and the communications zone, the zone piously insisting that when it came to supplies the troops came first, and the troops profanely accusing the zone of skimming off the cream. (For cream, read beer.) But there could be no question but that the POW camps got their supplies last."

About the only item that Korea had in plentiful supply at this particular time was scrap metal—the inevitable by-product of war's relentless waste. Necessity, therefore, became dam to a litter of inventions. The first vocational training facility to be installed in any camp was a forge; and each blacksmith shop multiplied itself just as rapidly as the tools could be fashioned. Going into the iron and steel business was accepted by the instructional staff as a means to an end: the theory was that more blacksmiths could make more tools to make more forges to train more blacksmiths, and so on. But the theory ran into an immediate snag—for cultural, rather than technical, reasons:

"Western and Eastern social systems clashed head-on... Neither the Chinese nor the Koreans employ anything remotely resembling the European apprentice system nor the American vocational school. The few blacksmiths among the POW's cheerfully made forges and tools and stoves, but they objected strenuously to making more blacksmiths. Theirs was an ancient and an honored skill, one to be handed down only with the greatest circumspection, from father to oldest son; if there was no son, to some fortunate lad who would be adopted and treated thenceforth as a son.

"They were not about to teach blacksmithing to ragtag, bobtail prisoners of war. And every other skilled artisan in the camps felt exactly the same way about passing on his specialty.

"Breaking down this attitude took some doing and was generally accomplished in this wise. The blacksmith was, of course, a prisoner of war and subject to military discipline. If the stubborn Americans insisted on permitting half a dozen men to watch him work, there was nothing he could do about it. If the Americans then ordered him away from his anvil, and let one of those men take his place, there was nothing he could do about that, either. But if the man who took his place miserably botched his attempt to imitate the blacksmith, as he usually did, pride of profession had the blacksmith in there showing him how to do it right, with the Americans and the class applauding. Suddenly he had a new status, one even more honorable than blacksmithing. He was a teacher. By the time the the directors of the rehabilitation project could equip him with a textbook on blacksmithing, something they did as quickly as possible, he was practically a scholar. If he could not read the manual, he could at least understand and appreciate and point to the illustrations."

Another vocational training project of high priority was tinsmithing. Next to expended cartridges and wrecked vehicles, the most bountiful product that war creates—in an American army, at least—is empty cans. With the aid of the blacksmiths' skills, POW artisans devised machinery for converting discarded cans into workable sheets of tin on a mass-production basis. One ingenious tinsmith fashioned an apparatus for removing the tops and bottoms of beer cans in a single operation. Another craftsman constructed an oversize wringer which turned out sheets of tin corrugated like a galvanized iron washboard.

Most of this output went into the manufacture of stovepipes for the homemade oil-drum heaters in the prisoners' quarters. Some of it, however, found its way into a lucrative sideline: toys. Practically every camp soon had a flourishing trade in model airplanes, ships, tanks, and other gadgets with UN personnel of the camp command and occasional visitors.

"Shoe repair and tailor shops were two more vocational projects with which the camp commanders never quarreled," said Hansen. "The POW's were clothed in salvaged U.S. shoes and fatigues, which come in two well-known sizes, too large and too small. As far as the generally smaller Chinese and Korean POW's were concerned, they were usually too large and had to be cut down. This did not present too much of a tailoring problem, but cutting down shoes was a major cobbling operation which involved almost complete remanufacture."

In addition to these projects, vocational activities were organized around to make use of whatever natural resources were available in the immediate vicinity of each camp. "One camp had clay near by, ideal for making brick, and developed a busy brick factory. Another, near a source of stone, trained stone-cutters and stone-masons, and its buildings were handsomely and warmly faced with stone. Several were near or incorporated within their boundaries sources of potter's clay and had ceramic shops and kilns which produced really attractive ware. Still another, with an Air Force dump near by, constructed a miniature factory which made rice bowls out of damaged aluminum wing tanks, for all of the camps in Korea."

But production for production's sake was not the aim of the rehabilitation project—despite the value of the objects and artifacts which the POW shops turned out. Instructors selected only those vocational projects which furthered the training aspects of the program. According to Colonel Hansen:

> "The purpose of the vocational program was the development of manual skills among the POW's that would aid in their self-support and in the reconstruction of their countries after their eventual release. It was assumed that providing opportunities to develop

work skills would tend to develop favorable attitudes toward the agency which provided the opportunity, the United Nations, and this assumption proved to be correct.

"Even the Communist POW's, fearful of the educational aspects of the program lest they be weaned away from their careful dialecticism, welcomed the vocational projects...

"It was the men who were not suited mentally for the literacy, orientation, or adult continuation programs who particularly benefited from the vocational training. The very Asian reluctance to accept apprentices made the attainment of any skill at any of the useful trades being taught an opportunity which would ordinarily have been hard to come by for these Chinese and Koreans, and they appreciated it. Although many of them returned to Red China and North Korea, there can be no question but that with their newfound ability to earn a better-than-average living even under the Communist system, they are less dedicated Communists today because the United Nations gave them a leg up."

This, then, was our American version of "brainwashing." No coercion, no intimidation, no calculated malnutrition, no Pavlovian conditioning, no relays of brutal inquisitors with endless questions. Merely an opportunity to live for a period of time—even behind barbed wire—in the clean air of freedom and to make use of whatever natural talents one has been given to learn, grow, and develop.

Did the program work?

The results speak for themselves. From one group among the Chinese POW's who refused repatriation to Red China, the following letter was sent to the men and women who had worked on the United Nations Command rehabilitation project:

"We wish to express our heartfelt gratitude to you... When we underwent the bitter life of imprisonment, you taught us, despite all hardships, how to read and write, carpentry and blacksmithing; you provided us with newspapers, radio broadcasts and movies in order to comfort us when we were lonely; and you invited many instructors and experts to explain to us the principles of democracy.

"During those three long years, you were our teachers and companions. You encouraged and comforted us, enabled us to gain knowledge and skill in handicrafts. You were most concerned about us when we were transferred to the demilitarized zone. Now we have returned to Taiwan victoriously. Representing the 14,343 anti-Communist brothers, we wish to pay you our highest respects...

"We have shaken ourselves free from the yoke of the Communists and returned to our fatherland. But we could not forget that Russian imperialism and its running dogs—Chu-Mao—are persecuting our countrymen on the mainland and paving the way to the enslavement of humanity. We hope that you will help us tell the world our experiences so that others shall not be cheated and trapped by the Communists.

"We don't understand why some statesmen still fall for Communist peace propaganda. If the Communist bandits were sincere in their desire for peace, why were we forced to go to Korea to fight? We have families on the China mainland; nevertheless, we, 14,343 anti-Communist brothers, have risked our lives and chosen to return to Taiwan, our free fatherland. The Chu-Mao bandits are still killing our people in order to maintain their dictatorial rule. They are our deadly enemies. Taiwan has become the lighthouse of freedom of the Chinese people on the mainland. And President Chiang is their beloved leader. We, here, appeal to the Free World to strengthen its unity and to cooperate with Free China in the sacred battle of anti-aggression and anti-slavery.

> "We again pay our respects to you for your untiring efforts in teaching us. We shall never cease to feel grateful for your help."

The message was signed: Representatives of the 14,343 Anti-Communist Brothers.

CHAPTER SIX

A Study in Scarlet

RED HAS ALWAYS BEEN A FAVORITE COLOR with the Chinese—for reasons that have nothing to do with politics. It is associated with gaiety and good luck; and, unless the Communists have succeeded in brainwashing the bulk of the population, the more superstitious among the Chinese still attribute magical significance to the color red. On the seventh day of each new lunar period, for example, friends are enjoined to stay at home and eat red beans—7 for the man and 14 for the woman—to ward off illness. Red candles were the traditional device for frightening away homeless ghosts.

Consequently, when some unidentified halfwit in epaulettes on the POW staff at Koje—acting from motives that bedraggle the imagination—saw fit to issue a summer gym suit consisting of T-shirt and shorts, dyed a brilliant RED, the Chinese prisoners accepted them without demur.

They were grateful, but mystified, no doubt. By this time the Chinese POW's were absolutely convinced—especially the fervent anti-Communists among them—that Americans are the maddest captors in the world. Fanatical Communists were equally mystified, but generosity—in their contemptuous view—merely demonstrated the softness of American heads, rather than American hearts. At any rate, it is not recorded that the Communist Chinese refused to accept the gaudy crimson sport costumes.

With the Korean prisoners, however, it was an entirely different story. Whoever gave the order for an issue of red shirts and shorts in the Korean compounds unwittingly touched off the first incident in Korea's civil war behind barbed wire. When the track suits were passed out, the Korean POW's promptly chucked them over the fence at their guards. "One Communist compound," according to William L. White, "took the extra precaution of wrapping them around large rocks. One of these flattened a South Korean MP, whereupon his colleagues, men of spirit and in no mood to take insults from Communists, in or out of prison...opened fire, killing three."

More trouble was on the way—in a packet tied with scarlet ribbons.

In the spring of 1951, the compounds at Koje were far from escape-proof, even when measured by indifferent standards. A few skimpy strands of barbed wire and a guard's rifle were all that separated a determined prisoner from the larger freedom of the island. If he happened to be Korean, it was a simple enough matter to doff his POW garb and seek refuge with one of the Korean families in the nearest Koje village. Next morning, dressed in white pantaloons and straw hat, he could strap an A-frame on his back and stroll past the compound without fear of being recognized.

That pesky uniform was a headache for the UN staff. As the Koje hills turned green with spring vegetation, a prisoner wearing U. S. Army fatigues was as good as outfitted in camouflage. He could simply drift away from a working party—or under the barbed wire—and melt into his surroundings.

The answer seemed to be obvious: more distinctive uniforms. With the time approaching for a new clothing issue, it seemed quite logical to dye them red. Said Colonel Hansen, "Red would stand out fine against the green hills. It was warm enough in the spring sunshine to line the men up, have them divest themselves of their greens and then move along the enclosure to the issue point in their underwear, there to receive bright new uniforms."

And that is where the trouble started.

While the few Chinese prisoners accepted them as readily as their comrades had accepted the red suits, not a single Korean prisoner—Communist or anti-Communist—would have anything to do with the new fatigues. Things were the same in every Korean compound. To the last man, they refused to receive the red uniforms.

The American commander of the camp was completely floored. He made a vain attempt to learn from the prisoners why they objected so vigorously to the new fatigues, but his queries met with stony silence. Communication was always a problem in the Korean compounds, but this was a situation without precedent. The Koreans were just not talking. Period. "To repeated questioning," said Hansen, "all the camp commander and his men got were the whites of the men's eyes." It was a ridiculous situation, but the commander refused to allow himself to be intimidated. Very well. If the prisoners refused to wear the new uniforms, they could damn well run around in their underwear.

Which is exactly what they did—at least for the next 10 days. By that time, the commander took recourse to an old Army solution: he went to see the chaplain. "This chaplain was not an Army officer," said Colonel Hansen, "or perhaps he would have come to the commander with the answer he was seeking. He was a missionary with long experience in Korea, and as puzzled as the prisoners at the commander's insistence that the men wear red uniforms."

"I wish you had asked me about it before you dyed the uniforms red," he told the commander. "During the Japanese occupation, when a criminal was condemned to death he was given a red uniform." Whether the chaplain was correct in assuming that the Koreans were convinced they were all going to be shot, red was the color of degradation—and that was enough for them.

So, the red uniforms were quietly put away, and green fatigues were issued at once—with apologies from the Koje commander. The anti-Communist POW's accepted the apologies in good spirit. But as far as the Communist prisoners were concerned, the damage was done. "They had learned," Colonel Hansen pointed out, "that a completely united compound could defy the U. S. command, and a year later they put that knowledge to use."

CHAPTER SEVEN

One-Star Hostage

TWENTY MILES NORTH OF SEOUL astride the M.S.R., the road which the U.S. Army logistics command has designated the Main Supply Route for the American and ROK divisions deployed along the military demarcation line, is the town of Uijong-bu. It was here, through this rent in the mountainous curtain drawn about the capital of the Republic of Korea, that the drab Communist legions of Kim Il Sung came spilling on June 25, 1950. Here, through the Uijongbu Corridor—traditional entry port for invaders from the north—rumbled the Soviet-built trucks, artillery, and T–34 tanks of the People's Democratic Army of North Korea.

Just outside Uijongbu is Camp Red Cloud. This small military compound, which was named for an American GI hero of Indian extraction, is headquarters today, as it was ten years ago, for U.S. Army First Corps. Since the end of the Korean war, the position of Chief of Staff for I Corps has been filled by a succession of officers whose tour of duty has averaged thirteen months. In the spring of 1952, the job was held by Brigadier General Charles F. Colson—whose assignment came to a much more abrupt end than most.

A decade has wrought few visible changes in the village of Uijong-bu, except to add a garish, unsightly strip of souvenir and trinket stalls, bars, pawn shops, cabarets, and brothels which cater to a flourishing GI trade. Store fronts which line the M.S.R. are mostly fashioned from flattened beer cans, and are decorated with handpainted signs which feature crude imitations of Stateside advertising eyewash in an amusing assortment of misspelled words. The reeking alleys are of mud macadamized with garbage and human ordure.

One of the few innovations since 1952 is a light plane landing strip near the camp. All day long there is a buzz of traffic as small L–19 Puddlejumpers take off and land, their flashing prop blades practically brushing the thatched roofs of huts in the village. A scant hundred yards or so away, behind stolid red oxen, Korean farmers till their rice paddies—oblivious to the roar of airplanes that swoop in low overhead on their final approach.

All in all, the scenery has changed very little since that day in May of 1952 when Charles F. Colson received an urgent message from the Eighth Army commander, General Van Fleet: Drop everything and report immediately to Koje-do...

Inside the barbed wire of Compound 76, General Frank Dodd was resting comfortably—albeit uneasily—in the apartment or "command post" his Red captors had thoughtfully provided. They had even gone to the trouble of making commissary arrangements with the POW camp command: meals from Dodd's own mess were sent in from outside.

Whatever the fates held in store for General Dodd, he would at least be spared the ordeal by hunger that another prominent American captive—General William Dean—was forced to endure at the hands of the Communists.

But chowtime brought its trials and tribulations. Meals were more robust than General Dodd's appetite, for there was no mistaking the foot-of-the-gallows air about the whole procedure. Dodd must have approached each mouthful of food with the unspoken thought: The condemned man ate a hearty meal.

Before departing for Koje Island, General Colson received a sketchy and hurried briefing—the only kind that the pressure of time permitted.

This was the first snarl in the tangled skein. Colson was walking into a complex, highly-charged situation which called for great skill and detailed knowledge of the events that had already taken place at Koje. Was General Colson aware, for example, that Communist agents, disguised as ordinary soldiers, had deliberately exposed themselves to capture for the purposes of infiltrating the UN compounds?

Charles F. Colson was a soldier, and a good one. A West Point graduate of the 1918 class that included Leslie R. Groves of Manhattan Project fame, Colson had led a combat command of the 8th Armored Division during World War II. Like his unlucky predecessor, General Colson was totally unfamiliar with the subtleties of Oriental political connivery.

When he arrived at Koje-do, Colson found that affairs had settled into an unstable equilibrium. The relative calm that had descended over the camp could be terminated explosively at a split-second's notice by an overt act of hostility from either side.

Compound 76 looked peaceful—almost deserted. The prisoners were staying under cover by order of their leaders, but the flags and signs were still very much in evidence.

Outside the barbed wire fence, U.S. troops patrolled the perimeter with fixed bayonets. Tanks were parked with their treads almost touching the rolls of concertina wire along the drainage ditches. Their 90 mm. cannon muzzles poked grimly toward the quonset huts in the center of the compound.

After consulting with the camp authorities, General Colson authorized the installation of a telephone extension to Compound 76. This had been an early Communist request. A telephone was passed through the barbed wire and connected to a sentry box at the main gate. Most of the subsequent negotiations were then carried on by this means.

In his first conversation with General Dodd, Colson learned that he had been treated well by the POW "high command." Dodd also relayed a Red demand that two Communist leaders from each of the compounds be permitted to enter Compound 76 for the purposes of attending a conference called by Senior Colonel Lee Hak Koo, the Red officer who appeared to be in charge of affairs. General Colson acceded to this demand, and the "representatives" strutted insolently into the compound. Getting them back out again would later prove a bit of a problem.

"The price for Dodd's freedom," said General Clark, "had been fixed by the prisoners in an outrageous set of demands they wanted Colson to sign. These included a promise that there would be no more forcible screening (to which of course we had never resorted) nor any nominal screening to determine which prisoners were willing to return to Communism and which ones were not. Such a commitment was tantamount to a field commander's changing the policy of his government, which in this case was to screen prisoners. The screening process had been established to implement our government's policy of refusing to force any prisoner back to Communism. The demands also were so worded that if accepted they would have constituted tacit admission of a whole list of trumped up crimes the Communists alleged the UN Command had committed against the prisoners."

Indeed, as General Clark pointed out, they were questions of the category: "Have you stopped beating your wife?"

These demands were written in Korean and signed by the "PW Representative Group of North Korean People's Army and Chinese People's Volunteer Army." The following is a copy of the translation which was handed to General Colson—complete with the mangled English of the original version:

"1. Immediate ceasing the barbarous behavior, insults, torture, forcible protest with blood writing, threatening, confine, mass murdering, gun and machine-gun shooting, using poison gas, germ weapons, experiment object of A-bomb, by your command. You should guarantee PW human rights and individual life with the base on the International Law.

"2. Immediate stopping the so-called illegal and unreasonable voluntary repatriation of North Korean Peoples Army and Chinese Peoples Volunteer Army PW.

"3. Immediate ceasing the forcible investigation [screening] which thousands of PW of North Korean Peoples Army and Chinese Peoples Volunteer be rearmed and falled in slavery, permanently and illegally.

"4. Immediate recognition of the PW Representative Group [Commission] consisted of North Korean Peoples Army and Chinese Peoples Volunteer Army PW and close cooperation to it by your command.

"This Representative Group will turn in Brig Gen Dodd, USA, on your hand after we receive the satisfactory written declaration to resolve the above items by your command. We will wait for your warm and sincere answer."

General Colson's "warm and sincere" answer will be recorded in its proper place in the sequence of negotiations. First, however, it is necessary to take a closer look at this Communist message.

Like most documents that originate with the Communists, the message was heavily saturated with propaganda.

Poison gas—as the Reds were perfectly well aware—had never been used at any time during the Korean conflict by either side. United

Nations guards had, on several occasions, employed tear gas grenades to quell mutinous prisoners.

The reference to "experiment object of A-bomb" was another Red canard. It involved the oft-quoted Communist charge that the UN Command had made guinea-pigs of Red prisoners of war in sinister atomic bomb experiments carried out near the Korean coast. The Communists repeated this nonsense with a straight face, both in the Red press and in the truce talks at Panmunjom. The original basis for such preposterous allegations apparently was derived from reports that the UN Command had used a hospital ship anchored off Pusan for the preparation of typhus serum—with which Communist troops incidentally, along with out own men, were impartially innoculated.

Germ-warfare charges constitute the "Big Lie" of the Korean conflict. Using a combination of starvation, isolation, and psychological intimidation, the Reds succeeded in extracting from captured American fliers a number of confessions that they had participated in vicious bacteriological attacks against the civilian population of North Korea. Despite the patent absurdity of these accusations, there were many people on both sides of the Iron Curtain who believed—and still believe—the truth of such assertions.

General Colson, however, should have known better.

The message containing the Communist POW demands was sent to Colson on the morning of May 10th—General Dodd's third day of captivity. On the previous day, there had been a near-explosion in Compound 76. The Reds had threatened to kill Dodd and stage a camp-wide uprising when rumors reached them that UN troops were about to attempt a crash rescue on May 9th. Dodd had advised Colson to hold off the attack.

Later, this piece of advice was used to disparage General Dodd's reputation—a thoroughly reprehensible and slanderous maneuver.

Frank Dodd had demonstrated his personal bravery on more than one battlefield, but he refused to stoop to the indignity of defending his actions or explaining his motives. As a matter of fact, he had advised against the attack to avoid bloodshed—not to save his own skin.

Colson had already informed the prisoners that he was willing to negotiate with a Communist grievance committee, presumably headed by Colonel Lee Hak Koo, who seemed to be in general charge of the compound. But he refused to make any promises about voluntary repatriation, since the matter was under discussion at Pan-munjom.

After his release, Dodd gave an account of what happened in Compound 76 on May 10th during the exchange of messages between the POW's and General Colson. Following the delivery of the four-point Red agenda, "There was the normal delay of translation, and General Colson immediately gave them a written answer. They studied this answer until noon. They then came to my tent and reported to me that the answer was entirely unsatisfactory. Actually, General Colson had agreed to their demands, but from their translation from English into Kwangji it was obvious that they did not understand this.

"I then modified General Colson's letter to their liking, and asked them if such a modified statement would be satisfactory. They informed me that it would. General Colson signed this statement and returned it to them promptly. However they then found minor corrections necessary, to which they attached considerable importance. It was, therefore, necessary to prepare a third statement. Colonel Lee Hak Koo had sent a written statement to General Colson that as soon as they had received a satisfactory statement signed by him and had an opportunity to read and understand it they would release me unharmed."

The text of the third or final statement General Colson signed to obtain Dodd's freedom is as follows:

"1. With reference to your Item 1 of that message, I do admit that there have been instances of bloodshed where many prisoners of war have been killed and wounded by UN Forces. I can assure you that in the future the prisoners of war can expect humane treatment in this camp according to the principles of International Law. I will do all within my power to eliminate further violence and bloodshed. If such incidents happen in the future, I will be responsible.

"2. Reference your Item 2, regarding voluntary repatriation of NKPA and CPVA prisoners of war, that is a matter which is being discussed at Panmunjom. I have no control or influence over the decisions at the Peace Conference.

"3. Regarding your Item 3 pertaining to forcible investigation [screening], I can inform you that after Gen. Dodd's release, unharmed, there will be no more forcible screening or any rearming of prisoners of war in this camp, nor will any attempt be made at nominal screening.

"4. Reference your Item 4, we approve the organization of a PW Representative Group or Commission consisting of NKPA and CPVA prisoners of war, according to the details agreed by Gen Dodd and approved by me."

"I am furnishing this reply in writing over my signature as requested by you, through Gen Dodd with the understanding that upon the receipt of this reply you will release Gen Dodd, unharmed, as soon as possible, but under no circumstances later than 8 o'clock p.m. this date. Signed:

Charlie F. Colson, Brig Gen USA
Commanding General

Since this document was later used as the principal basis for instituting board action against General Colson, it is imperative to examine more closely what he actually said.

First he said: "I do admit that there have been instances of bloodshed where many prisoners of war have been killed and wounded by UN Forces." As literal truth, this statement can scarcely be challenged: POW's *had* been killed by UN guards at Koje-do. Unaware that he was writing for publication in the Communist press, Colson apparently didn't feel it was necessary to qualify his remarks by adding that the prisoners had been killed while rioting against the just and lawful orders of the camp command.

Colson also promised that "in the future the prisoners of war can expect humane treatment" in the camp "according to the principles of International Law." Unless General Colson had been thoroughly briefed in preparation for his assumption of command at Koje Island, it is not unreasonable to assume that he was largely ignorant of the lenient UN policy which had been in effect at Koje for many months. And as the new camp commander, Colson was completely within his authority in promising the POW's to do anything possible to eliminate further violence and bloodshed.

General Colson's response to the second demand—regarding the voluntary repatriation issue—was perfectly correct. He refused to accept any responsibility for matters that were outside his sphere of authority as Koje camp commandant. In the very next paragraph, however, Colson does precisely that when he agrees to put an end to "forcible screening" and "rearming prisoners of war"—neither of which had ever taken place within the United Nations POW command.

This was the critical item in Colson's reply, and it is probably the one that cost him his command and his star. For in extending a promise to the Reds to halt screening operations, General Colson had overstepped his authority. The interesting question is: Why did Colson agree to this demand?

In the absence of any statement by General Colson[1] his reason or reasons can only be a matter for speculation. It is difficult, however to escape the conviction that Colson was not fully informed by his own superiors regarding the gravity of the voluntary repatriation issue. If this were the case, he would probably be persuaded to weigh it lightly against General Dodd's life.

At any rate, Colson sent another and much more peremptory message to the rebels of Compound 76:

> "1. You have treacherously seized and are illegally holding Brigadier General Frank Dodd. General Dodd is no longer in command of the U.N. POW enclosure, and has no authority for any decisions or actions...
>
> "2. You are directed to release him by 10 AM Saturday. If this is not done, all necessary force will be taken to effect his release, regardless of consequences to you..."

The Communists ignored the deadline. They made one more effort to squeeze some propaganda value from their possession of General Dodd. According to Dodd, after the prisoners had already agreed to turn him loose on the strength of Colson's assurances, they then postponed the release claiming that the weather was so bad that they would hold him until morning.

"I then discovered," said Dodd, "that they had prepared another letter to General Colson informing him of the arrangements for the release ceremony. Apparently I was to be decorated in flowers and escorted to the gate between formed lines of PWs.

"I was to be met at the gate by General Colson where I would be delivered into his custody. I informed them that we could call the whole matter off, that they had not lived up to their promises, that they had admitted that General Colson's statement was satisfactory and now they wished to place other unacceptable conditions upon my release.

"I informed them that if they could not live up to their promises we would not live up to ours. By this time it was 9 o'clock May 10th. They immediately agreed that I was right and requested that I inform General Colson that I would be released at 9:30. There was some further discussion about the possibility of the removal of the troops in order that I might depart in a peaceful atmosphere. This I refused to discuss. They then agreed to arrange for my release at 9:30 and at this time I was delivered to the gate by the principal leaders and released."

Among the latter was an unidentified prisoner with no indications of any commissioned rank. Nevertheless, he was obviously a personage of importance—the "commissar of the entire camp," as one report put it. Even the chief of Compound 76, Colonel Lee, deferred to the "private" who wielded such powerful influence.

It was, of course, Pak Sang Hyong.

Thus, on May 10, 1952, eleven and a half hours after Colson's deadline, and 78 hours after his abduction, Brigadier General Francis T. Dodd USA walked out the gate of Compound 76 to where the men of his staff were awaiting his return. General Colson stepped forward and shook his hand. Then the two officers climbed into a jeep and headed back to the POW camp command headquarters.

The mutiny at Koje-do was over—for the time being.

CHAPTER EIGHT

Generals Three

On the very day that General Dodd was seized at Koje-do, the United Nations Command was in the process of changing hands—a situation fraught with unfortunate implications for the rapidity with which UN authorities were liable to react to the situation in the POW camps. General Matthew B. Ridgway, who had already been named as the new NATO commander in Europe, was about to hand over the UN Command to his successor, General Mark W. Clark, when the Koje-do mutiny broke out. His immediate response was to delay his departure for Washington long enough to brief General Clark on the entire range of Far Eastern developments.

Time did not permit Ridgway to do more than sketch the background of the Koje-do mutiny. En route to Korea for a conference with General Van Fleet, Commander of the Eighth U. S. Army, Ridgway brought up the incident at Koje. Said Clark:

> "I woke up next morning eager to get on the job. I drove to the airport and met Ridgway. After takeoff he said to me:
>
> "'Wayne, we've got a little situation over in Korea where it's reported some prisoners have taken in one of the camp Commanders, General Dodd, and are holding him as a hostage. We'll have to get into that situation when we arrive at Eighth Army Headquarters and find out what the score is.'"

The score, according to Clark's acrid commentary, was "exactly no hits, no runs, and more errors than any scorekeeper would have the heart to tally."

As Ridgway discussed the Dodd kidnapping, Clark—he later admitted—"got the feeling I was walking into something that felt remarkably like a swinging door. This was astounding news to me, something for which I had no preparation whatever. Although I had been briefed in Washington on every conceivable subject, this was the first time I had ever heard of Koje or the critical prisoner-of-war problem that existed behind our lines."

One can only sympathize with General Clark. Even at this point, more than ten years later, it seems almost incredible that the officer designated as the next Supreme Commander for the Far East should be allowed to depart for his new assignment in total ignorance of a situation which was apt to become his most pressing problem. But this is precisely what had happened to Mark Clark. By the time the reasons for this startling default in critical intelligence communication became apparent, they had ceased to be of more than academic importance.

From General Van Fleet in Seoul, Ridgway received a report on the latest developments in the Dodd affair—with General Clark looking over his shoulder. Van Fleet, a West Point classmate of Eisenhower and Bradley, was a tough, aggressive combat leader with an outstanding record in three wars. In 1948 he was sent to Greece as a military adviser and helped the Greek Army win its long war against the Communist guerrillas. Since taking over the 8th Army from Ridgway a year earlier, Van Fleet had done a superlative job in maintaining the aggressive spirit and combat skill of his soldiers under the most adverse and trying circumstances.

It was evident to Clark, however, that Van Fleet's duties were far too extensive and detailed: "He ran the war on a 155-mile front, the complicated liaison with the South Korean Government, and was finally responsible for the security of prisoners of war, supplies, communications, and everything that happened from the battle line all the way back to Pusan, which meant the whole of South Korea."[1]

From Van Fleet, Clark and Ridgway learned for the first time the arrogant demands the Red POW's were making in bargaining for Dodd's release. "They insisted that they be allowed to form a vast prisoner-of-war association, complete with bylaws and an intercompound telephone, and be provided with additional tents, desks, chairs, reams and reams of paper, ink, fountain pens, mimeograph machines and even two three-quarter ton trucks!"

Not quite 24 hours had elapsed since Dodd was whisked away into the recesses of Compound 76. There was the urgent matter of a replacement for the captured POW camp commander. Ridgway gave instructions for the appointment of a successor to Dodd; and later that day, after visiting I Corps Headquarters near Uijongbu Clark learned that Van Fleet had selected Brigadier General Charles F. Colson, I Corps Chief of Staff, to take over the POW command at Koje-do.

Next stop on the Ridgway-Clark itinerary was Munsan-ni, a village near Panmunjom. There the two officers met with Vice Admiral Joy for a conference on the progress—or rather the lack of it—that the UN delegation was making in the truce negotiations. Clark described Admiral Joy as "absolutely flabbergasted" by the Dodd kidnapping. Later, Admiral Joy himself, in his book *How Communists Negotiate*, stated: "Of all 'incidents' by which the Communists sought to gain advantages, none was so bloody nor so successful as the Koje-do riots... By instigating a violent revolt...the Communists created an atmosphere which greatly jeopardized the major position of our delegation in the armistice conference—that relating to the exchange of prisoners."

Ridgway had also arranged for staff officers from the 8th Army to meet him at Munsan-ni with further information for a more detailed report on what was taking place at Koje-do. The report was far from optimistic. Said Clark:

"We didn't even know exactly how many prisoners were on the island, for *the fanatical Communists hadn't permitted our authorities inside some compounds for many months* [Italics mine]. Therefore our camp officials had been unable to count their prisoners.

"The best figure Eighth Army could give Ridgway was 80,000 which was an approximation. At the time the report was compiled at Munsan-ni, these prisoners were at the height of their 'victory demonstration.' They were in open defiance of their guards. They flew Communist flags, strung insulting English-language banners on the barbed wire of their enclosures, and mounted barracks rooftops to wigwag signals from one compound to another, and to shout insults at our guards. They evidenced no disposition to release Dodd.

"The Communist leaders inside the compounds had whipped up a spirit of fervent fanaticism among the prisoners. The capture of Dodd fed the POW's the kind of success and excitement needed to make them feel exultant and ready to do battle."

In his conference with General Van Fleet, Ridgway discovered that he was planning to negotiate with the Red POW leaders for Dodd's release. This procedure was thoroughly unacceptable to Ridgway, and he expressed his objections in the most emphatic terms.

Admiral Joy, on the other hand, convinced by his months of daily exposure to Communist deceit, arrogance, and bullying that the Reds were responsive solely to the language of naked force, fully concurred with Ridgway's estimate of the situation. He felt that Dodd's immediate release should be demanded, and that this demand should be backed up with an impressive show of strength. As Ridgway said later in his report to President Truman: "I then directed Van Fleet, in writing, to establish order in the prison camps immediately and thereafter to maintain it, and to use whatever force was necessary. This order required the movement of a battalion of tanks of the 3rd Division two hundred miles by road from their position in the north, and their transshipment by LST across to the island. I was determined that if the Red POW's made any resistance, or attempted any delay in carrying out our demands, we would shoot, and I wanted the killing machinery on hand to do a thorough job of it."

From 8th Army Headquarters in Seoul, General Ridgway sent off a report to Washington—his first report—on the Koje outbreak. In it he included the directives he had given to General Van Fleet which authorized him to proceed *at once* against the Koje rebels. Speed was stressed in these orders; and Van Fleet was covered from any potential criticism from Washington by the full authority of General Ridgway in the event it became necessary to use violence to rescue Dodd. How these orders were carried out will be seen shortly.

Ridgway's report to Washington stated that the UN contingent on Koje Island numbered more than eleven thousand troops, one-third of them soldiers of the ROK Army. Together with the tank battalion which had already been dispatched and another regiment of infantry, the Koje garrison was nearing the proportions of a miniature Army. In spite of this impressive military array, Ridgway's report continued, the staff intelligence officer on Koje-do had expressed the opinion that the POW's were capable of capturing the island itself.

General Clark listened to this evaluation with open mouth. To him, the assertion that a group of prisoners, however large, could overcome nearly a full division of well-armed and well-trained combat veterans, supported by a company of medium tanks, was arrant nonsense. Besides—there was a further point to consider. Supposing that some sizable portion of prisoners broke out of their compounds, where did this intelligence officer expect them to go?

On the following day, May 9, it was time to return to Tokyo. Protocol, however, called for an official visit with President Syngman Rhee in Pusan. "This was my first meeting," said Clark, "with the man who has been called the George Washington of Korea—and a lot of other things. The meeting was perfunctory. Matt said goodbye and President Rhee welcomed me cordially, assuring me that as the new United Nations Commander I would receive the same support from his splendid forces as had my predecessor."

Before winging out over the Sea of Japan, Ridgway and Clark instructed the pilot of their C–54 to swoop in low over the island of Koje so that Clark could take a closer look at the layout of the POW camp. From the air everything looked peaceful.

It was the second day of General Dodd's captivity.

General Van Fleet chose May 9 to make the second of his two trips to Koje-do. Colson had already entered into negotiations with the prisoners for Dodd's release. "It was a rough situation," General Clark acknowledged. "It was not made easier for Colson by frequent telephone conversations with Dodd inside the compound, which subjected Colson to added psychological pressure. In this way the prisoners used Dodd to argue their case. Among other things they told Dodd that if efforts were made to rescue him by force the prisoners would kill him."

Back in Tokyo, Ridgway was trying to keep one eye on the Koje situation, take care of the million and one details required in preparation for the transfer of command to General Clark, and maintain communication with Washington. Said Clark: "I was on the sidelines at this juncture but was filled in on every move because in only a few hours the Dodd incident would be my baby. My feeling was that we should have gone in with force to release Dodd... I am convinced that if there had been bloodshed it would have been mostly Communist blood. Of one thing I was certain. You don't negotiate with prisoners of war, particularly fanatical Communist PWs who consider themselves combatants despite capture. At best, negotiation with prisoners is a losing game."

On May 12, 1952, General Ridgway passed the reins to Mark Clark and took off for the United States. When he later briefed President Truman on the Koje affair, he was happy to report that Dodd had been turned loose by the Reds: "As it turned out, the use of force was not necessary. Once it became clear to the Communists that we were resolved to back up our demands, General Dodd was released and the situation settled down. In my view, the whole situation had been ineptly handled by the responsible officers in Korea."

With all due respect to General Ridgway, these statements add up to so much pontifical hooey. Unless Ridgway was speaking from complete ignorance, he should have known that it wasn't a United Nations show of force that got Frank Dodd out of his barbed wire coop, but the document that General Colson signed at Communist dictation. It was UN concessions, not bayonets, that opened the gate of Compound 76.

Ridgway's second point is better taken. There can be little doubt that "the whole situation had been ineptly handled." And although Ridgway hesitated to name names, who better fits the designation of "responsible officer" than the 8th Army commander, General Van Fleet?

Van Fleet was on the spot, armed with all the authority necessary to send up to 12,000 UN soldiers, armed to the teeth and backed up by tanks, into Compound 76 after Dodd. Ridgway's message had underlined the necessity for speed. Yet Van Fleet issued no orders to move against the compound. Instead, negotiations dragged on as "minor concessions by both sides postponed almost hour by hour the order to rescue Dodd forcibly. This was interpreted—and correctly—by the Communists," said Clark, "as a sign of weakness on our part."

And the responsibility for this "sign of weakness" falls squarely on nobody else than General Van Fleet—something which was conveniently forgotten when the time came later to festoon Dodd and Colson with a dead cat apiece. Van Fleet could have—should have—given the order to break into Compound 76, not General Colson. As the senior officer on the spot, it was clearly Van Fleet's place to issue the appropriate orders. Instead, Van Fleet appears to have restricted himself to a bit of exalted brooding—leaving Charles F. Colson holding the bag.

CHAPTER NINE

For Want of a Nail

"WHAT SHOULD BRIGADIER GENERAL FRANCIS T. DODD have done when the Communist prisoners on Koje Island seized him?" asked the writer of a feature article on the Koje mutiny in one of the news magazines.

The answer—to a certain ripsnorting, firebreathing, two-star denizen of the Pentagon—was perfectly obvious. From a well-entrenched position behind his desk nameplate, secured in flank and rear by his public relations staff, this brass hat loosed a barrage against the former Koje commander. Speaking "strictly off the record," it was his opinion that, as soon as Dodd was able to reach General Colson by telephone, he should have said: "Come in and get me, Charlie. Use all the guns and troops you need. If the Communist bastards kill me, the hell with it."

And General Colson?

Even if Dodd had made no such demand, the Pentagon officer said, Colson should have smashed his way into the compound with all the force at his disposal. The day would have been saved; the reputation of the U.S. Army would have been preserved untarnished; and Colson and Dodd would have been acclaimed as heroes. (In which case General Dodd's widow, presumably, could have made whatever arrangements were customary to accept his posthumous decoration.)

Unfortunately, things look different down on the line of scrimmage than they do to a Monday morning quarterback. Instead of a single dead hero, the Army had two live, very much discomfited, but exceedingly handy scapegoats.

For Frank Dodd and Charlie Colson, the nightmare that was the Koje-do mutiny did not come to an end with Dodd's release; the worst of the ordeal was still ahead.

The Communists wasted no time in turning the Koje affair to good account. Newspapers in Red China carried headlines about the American General who had openly confessed to United Nations "atrocities" against Communist POW's. At Panmunjom, the Dodd case came up almost daily in the deadlocked truce discussions. Red negotiators—and especially Nam Il—extracted every last bit of propaganda value from the document General Colson had signed to effect Dodd's release. According to Admiral Joy, "This paper said in effect that there would be no *more* forced screening, no *more* terrorization of the prisoners. This was the ammunition needed by the Communist delegation. Listen to them use it:

"GENERAL NAM IL: The former commandant of your prisoner-of-war camp openly admitted that your side used all sorts of violence to screen our captured personnel by force in an attempt to retain them as your cannon fodder. The newly appointed commandant of your prisoner-of-war camp openly implied to our captured personnel that no *further* criminal activities in violation of the Geneva Conventions would be perpetrated. Is it not a fact that your side, in order to carry out forcible screening, committed all kinds of atrocities, even including mass massacre against our captured personnel in disregard of the Geneva Conventions and repudiating the minimum standard of human behavior? Is it not a fact that the commandant of your prisoner-of-war camp promised our captured personnel that: 'There will be *no more* forcible screening?' You cannot deny these facts."

And a few days later, there was another broadside against Admiral Joy and his staff:

"GENERAL NAM IL: To release and repatriate all war prisoners in the custody of both sides after the cessation of hostilities is a matter of course; and is also explicitly required by the Geneva Convention. If this self-evident principle is followed, the question of war prisoners should have been settled speedily and reasonably long ago. The reason why the question of war prisoners is not yet settled is entirely due to your insistence on the absurd proposition of retaining our captured personnel as your cannon fodder, against the natural desire of war prisoners to return home to lead a peaceful life, and against the stipulation of the Geneva Convention as recognized by the whole world.

"In order to reach your objective of forcibly retaining our captured personnel, your side has long since used Chiang Kai-shek's gangsters and Syngman Rhee's agents to maltreat our captured personnel—employing every barbarous method and even creating world-known bloodshed to screen our captured personnel by force and subject them to your slavery. Your criminal acts against the law and against humanity have developed to such a notorious extent that they are impossible for you to hide.

"You should know that your proposition of retaining our captured personnel by force under the name of 'voluntary repatriation' is itself in total violation of the Geneva War Prisoner Convention. Your such unilateral and unreasonable proposition is absolutely unacceptable. Your side disregards the urgent desire of your own captured personnel to go home and lead a peaceful life. Your side chooses to insist upon your proposition of retaining our captured personnel rather than stopping the Korean War."

On May 21, there was still more of the same:

"GENERAL NAM IL: Your side has not yet made any account for the repeated massacre of our captured personnel perpetrated by your side. Yet your side once again carried out bloody murder of our captured personnel. The serious sanguinary incident of May 20th, in which your side inflicted eighty-six casualties among our barehanded, captured personnel in your prisoner-of-war camp at Pusan, once again exposed before the whole world that your so-called voluntary repatriation and screening are a great hoax and your so-called respect for 'fundamental human rights' and 'personal dignity' and 'humane principles' is a big lie.

"After your design to retain our captured personnel by force collapsed in bankruptcy, you have taken a series of measures of terror against them to retrieve your bankrupt design.

"It is obvious that you have overestimated the ability of the Chiang Kai-shek gangsters and Syngman Rhee's agents in coercing our captured personnel. You have underestimated the struggle and the unbending will of resistance of our captured personnel.

"In order to manufacture the so-called results of screening, your side directly prompted the Chiang Kai-shek and Syngman Rhee agents to coerce our captured personnel into tattooing their own bodies, writing blood petitions, and finger-printing. Your special agents mauled and beat our captured personnel unconscious and then dipped their hands in their own blood to put their fingerprints on your lists of so-called 'Prisoners of War Resisting Repatriation.'"

To this heavy North Korean and Chinese Red cannonade was added a popgun report: the U. S. Communist Party National Committee in New York announced it had sent President Truman a telegram denouncing the "bestial massacre" of POW's on Koje-do and demanding that the United Nations Security Council order the "immediate investigation and punishment of those responsible."

In addition to the Communist fusillade, Colson and Dodd shortly found themselves under a crossfire from the United Nations neutral press. One American newspaper called the Dodd kidnapping the "prize bumble of the year," and the concessions made by Colson "grossly humiliating" to the United States. A British journal suggested that the two officers be given "a special booby prize." All over the free world, people were commenting bitterly on the glaring deficiencies in political sense among U. S. military leaders that the Koje incident revealed.

The American people were especially aroused to learn the details of the POW setup on Koje—the "Alcatraz of Korea," as one magazine put it:

> "Equipment valued at millions of dollars was furnished by the Americans to keep the Communists happy. This includes U. S. type clothing worth 9 million. There are recreation huts, auditoriums, and public-address systems to provide music and entertainment. Supplies of soap, cigarettes and other things far surpasses anything that most Chinese prisoners have ever seen.
>
> "Prisoners often traded this equipment with local townspeople for watches, cigarette lighters, rings, even jewelry. Communists 'art craft' supplies donated by Americans to paint propaganda signs and letter leaflets denouncing the West."

While there is much in this account that is true, there is also much that is misleading. The article fails to specify that most of the facilities at Koje were fashioned by the POW's themselves from scrap lumber, discarded oil drums, beer cans, and other kinds of junk; and that such things as athletic equipment and radio parts were procured from U. S. Army salvage. More serious is the omission of any mention in the article of the fact that most of these improvements were made in compounds dominated by anti-Communist prisoners. For the most part, the fanatical Reds disdained American assistance and refused to expend any efforts on self-improvement.

Violence was recurrent among the prisoners; and on the two occasions when it erupted on a massive scale, UN guards were operating "under instructions originated by General Matthew B. Ridgway to avoid shooting except in actual [self] defense." The following month a dozen more rioters were killed. Communist leaders invited reprisals in an effort to obtain propaganda material, but their attempts were frustrated by the reluctance of the United Nations Command to punish the Communist clique.

"Kid glove treatment," according to the article, went even further:

"The island, a fourth smaller than Staten Island, N. Y., had a local civilian population of about 46,000, and many of these people apparently were in contact with the prisoners, performing services for the 'high command'...

"The prisoners themselves were not always confined to their barbed wire compounds. Work details, 'screened' by the Communists, and sometimes totalling hundreds of men, were permitted to go through town and over most of the island, under a token guard. Many of these groups brought back rocks for construction projects —rocks often used in violence among prisoners."

On May 12, the day after his release, General Dodd was flown to Eighth Army Headquarters near Seoul for what *Time* magazine called "a thorough chewing-out" by General Van Fleet. Dodd's session with Van Fleet seems to have been something less than abrasive, for General Clark later received a message from Van Fleet in which he generally concurred with what Dodd had to say about the Koje episode.

At this awkward and critical juncture—as we have seen earlier—

the UN command was in the process of turnover. General Clark was easily the busiest and most harrassed officer in the Far East:

"During the two days after Dodd's release I was briefed from morning to night on every aspect of the command, the battle and armistice talks in Korea, the political position of Japan, the defense of Japan, the disposition of troops, the enemy situation in Korea and all manner of broad subjects such as the political and economic situation in Korea.

"The second morning after Dodd's release [the twelfth] I was sitting at Matt Ridgway's desk in the Dai Ichi Building in Tokyo prior to the actual assumption of command, scheduled to take place as his plane left Haneda that afternoon. The telephone rang. It was Matt. Would I, he asked, please formally take over at 10:00 A.M. instead of at the 3:00 P.M. take-off time? Earlier in the week Matt had asked me when I wanted to take command and I laughed that 'in view of this POW situation maybe I'd better wait a couple of months.' I still felt that way when Matt asked me to take over five hours early so he could handle all the last minute chores of moving. My honest preference was to catch a plane myself and get out fast, but I agreed that a few hours one way or the other wouldn't matter.

"During the Honor Guard farewell ceremony, I whispered to Matt that I felt it essential a statement be released. I slipped a copy into his hand and told him to radio me his views on it right after takeoff.

"Matt walked up the plane ramp with his wife, his two-year-old son and a broad smile on his face. As he waved good-by, I visualized him throwing me a blazing forward pass. Within minutes after takeoff I received a message from the plane that he concurred in my proposed press release and felt it was necessary."

What Dodd had to say was eagerly awaited by the press. As Clark noted, "The lid was still on the Dodd-Colson business and the press sniping had turned into a barrage...(Dodd) had not been permitted to see reporters and the Colson ransom note still had not been made public thirty-six hours after the bare announcement that Dodd was free. The press was clamoring to get the full story from him, from Eighth Army, from anybody."

After his conference with Van Fleet, General Dodd was permitted an audience with the press. In this interview no questions were allowed from the reporters; Dodd merely read off a prepared statement which was mainly a factual account of his experiences while a captive of the Reds. Unfortunately, the statement concluded with the remark that "the demands made by the PWs are inconsequential and the concessions granted by the camp authorities were of minor importance."

During the next several days and weeks, General Dodd was to experience, on more than one occasion, bitter regret for having made this remark.

There was no question, of course, of restoring Dodd to command at Koje—nor elsewhere in Korea, for that matter. What would happen to General Colson, who had given the Communists such a handsome piece of propaganda with his acknowledgment of "instances of bloodshed," was not immediately apparent.

General Clark had been highly critical of the Eighth Army's suppression of the Dodd story, for press censorship was directly contrary to his own well-established policies on news coverage. On more than one occasion during World War II, in Africa and later as Fifth Army Commander in Italy, Clark had taken newsmen into his confidence and entrusted them with items of a classified nature. "Never once," said Clark, "did a single newsman betray my confidence." Better still, when it was impossible for Clark to release a story—for security or other reasons—news correspondents accepted the situation and withheld any critical comments.

It is unfortunate, therefore, that Clark did not replace Ridgway a few weeks earlier. Much of the significance of the Dodd incident would otherwise have been minimized.

The text of General Clark's press release sketched the background of the Koje insurrections and the details of Dodd's capture. Clark also quoted the demands made by the POW's and the statements contained in Colson's agreement. Then Clark denounced the entire transaction and repudiated the terms of the Colson agreement:

> "The reply by General Colson to the Communist prisoners was made under great duress at a time when the life of General Dodd was at stake. The Communist demands were unadulterated blackmail and any commitments made by General Colson as a result of such demands should be interpreted accordingly.
>
> "That the allegations set forth in the first demand of the Communist prisoners are wholly without foundation is indicated by the fact that the prisoners subsequently agreed to eliminate these allegations from their original message. The baseless charges concerning germ warfare already have been refuted by my predecessor, and I can state unequivocally that the United Nations has at no time engaged in any such illegal type of warfare.
>
> "Any violence that has occurred at Koje-do has been the result of the deliberate and planned machinations of unprincipled Communist leaders whose avowed intent has been to disrupt the orderly operation of the camp and to embarrass the UNC in every way possible.
>
> "It is obvious that these demonstrations were motivated by attempts to influence the Armistice negotiations. It has been equally obvious from the very start that the riots we have had were carefully

plotted and deliberately instigated by hard-core Communist leaders.

"The provisions of the Geneva Convention have been observed in the administration of UN POW Camp 1 at Koje-do. The few incidents which have resulted in bloodshed were deliberately instigated by Communist prisoners of war and the force employed by the UNC in connection with these incidents was for the purpose of restoring order and control.

"Representatives of the International Committee of the Red Cross have had access to the camp at all times, have visited every compound on the island and have talked to numerous prisoners. Many correspondents have visited the island in the past and have reported to the world on all aspect of the prisoners' lives."

It is distressing to have to add that General Clark was criticized in some irresponsible quarters for "reneging" on Colson's promises to the Communists. Only the Reds, it appeared, could violate their covenants with impunity.

General Clark had relieved Colson on May 14. A board of officers was shortly convened by the Eighth Army to investigate the matter of responsibility for the Dodd abduction. Clark was amazed to learn that Colson, in the opinion of the board members, was found to have "displayed coolness and excellent judgment" in his conduct of negotiations with the Red POW leaders. Further, it was their recommendation that no blame should be placed on General Dodd for being seized.

These results left General Van Fleet far from satisfied. He immediately forwarded to Clark his recommendation for administrative action against both officers. "By this time," said General Clark, "there was a crossfire from another direction... Army Secretary Pace, General Bradley, the Joint Chiefs of Staff, everybody in Washington was frantically calling for action. It was bad enough to have the Koje incident thrown in my lap, but it was made doubly difficult by the way Washington put on the pressure for immediate action."

On May 21, Clark set up another board of inquiry headed by Major General Blackshear M. Bryan—who later joined the UN truce delegation at Panmunjom—to make a final report to the Army on the Dodd kidnapping. The results of this second board proceedings were made public on May 23, when Secretary of the Army Frank Pace, Jr. announced to the press that Colson and Dodd had been demoted to the rank of Colonel and reassigned to duty in Japan—Dodd to the 16th U. S. Army Corps in Sendai, Colson to the U. S. Army Logistical Command.

General Clark has stated that Washington wanted "someone's head on a pike." That demand had now been fulfilled. Two career U. S. Army officers had become casualties of the Korean war just as surely as if they had fallen under a hail of Communist bullets.

But that was not the end of the story.

After remaining only a few days in Japan, Dodd and Colson were ordered back to Washington where, in the early part of June, they appeared before the House Armed Services Committee.

In statements made public on June 10, Colson and Dodd defended their agreement with Dodd's POW captors as having been in line with United Nations policy on the handling of prisoners at that time. Colson said he "fully expected these statements (that the UN had mistreated POW's) would be emphatically refuted, explained and shown to have been made under duress." Dodd said he felt "justified in assuming that large scale bloodshed (to force his release) was unacceptable."

Ever since assuming command at Koje on February 20, Dodd related, he found himself under what to him were strange orders. The prisoners, on instructions emanating from the Pentagon, were to be pampered, soothed, appeased—to make the truce talks run smoothly. Despite riots, frequent disturbances and open defiance, Dodd carried out these orders to the best of his ability until he was captured.

Colson—whom it is difficult to perceive as more than an innocent bystander in this ruction—was conscious of a basic conflict in his orders. On the one hand, he was to use whatever force might be needed for the purpose of releasing Dodd. But on the other hand, there was the standing general policy of lenient treatment of prisoners.

As a magazine article pointed out, "Colson's background did not include the intricacies of international politics. He perhaps was unaware that some Communists had become prisoners deliberately in order to foment troubles in the prison camps. He was taken in..."

The article pointed out that, "behind the Koje episode, critical observers find a reason for many U. S. troubles in Korea. Communist officers are trained, not only in war, but also in politics and propaganda. American military men know how to fight, but little of politics. So, in a war that has become more politics than fighting, the Communists have outmatched the American leaders."

On the very same day, June 10, a noncommissioned officer named Dean Chase, of Salt Lake City, said in Fort Ord, California, that he had been ordered court martialled because he wrote General Clark a "private and personal" letter in which he assailed Clark's repudiation of the deal for Dodd's release as "repugnant and disgraceful." Sergeant Chase stated that he was charged with showing disrespect to a superior officer, a violation of the 89th article of war.

Another recent returnee to what the Army calls the ZI—the "Zone of the Interior"—had also made an appearance before a Congressional body. General Ridgway was summoned for questioning by the

Senate Armed Services Committee. Members included Senators Russell, Bridges, Stennis and Morse. The following is an excerpt of General Ridgway's answers to questions put to him by the Chairman of the Armed Services Committee, Senator Richard B. Russell:

"SENATOR RICHARD B. RUSSELL, *Chairman, Armed Services Committee:* Was it ever brought to your attention, General Ridgway, that the more extreme Communists were exercising control over the internal operations of that prisoner compound [in Koje]?

"GENERAL MATTHEW B. RIDGWAY: Repeatedly, sir. The feeling was that the men, the actual company officers within the various compounds, were not the actual men who were directing these activities.

"SENATOR RUSSELL: How did camp commanders communicate with the people who were directing the Communists?

"GENERAL RIDGWAY: They did not, sir, they did not even know who they were—the usual Communist technique. That was reported to me repeatedly, sir.

"SENATOR RUSSELL: Were there any reports that came to your attention of the more fanatical Communists perpetrating any atrocities on those who were, perhaps, lukewarm or anti-Communists in the camp?

"GENERAL RIDGWAY: Yes sir; there were cases there where dead bodies would be found in the morning, under circumstances of death of those men which were never ascertained. They were unquestionably, in my opinion, just killed by direction of the fanatical Communists who, in fact, control the prisoners within the compound.

"SENATOR RUSSELL: What steps were taken, if any, to cure that condition?

"GENERAL RIDGWAY: *I could not answer accurately* [italics mine]. Every measure was taken, I believe, that those responsible officers thought they could take without resorting to measures which would have produced a lot of bloodshed.

"SENATOR RUSSELL: Was any effort made to segregate the people whose lives would be in danger, and get them away from this danger?

"GENERAL RIDGWAY: That was an inseparable element in the whole problem of screening—to find out those whose lives were in danger, and to get them out. That involved breaking up these large compounds, which were undesirably large, into much smaller groups, and the alternatives that faced the Eighth Army were these: The best form of prisoner-of-war guard, in the judgment of the Eighth Army, was either U.S. troops or European troops, because there was so much fanatical ill will between these Communist prisoners, particularly the North Korean prisoners, and the South Korean military guards."

So a decision had to be made as to how much combat strength could be safely diverted from the front to guard these prisoner-of-war camps. We had a very large concentration, as you know, on that one island.

To have broken them up into small sizes would have been desirable, but would have greatly increased the requirements for overhead of guards and prisoner-of-war camp administration.

So, up until the time that we were faced with the necessity of doing this, General Van Fleet's... decision was to retain that mass of prisoners-of-war in the one location, that one island.

In the passages quoted above, Ridgway tacitly apportions the responsibility for the POW disturbances equally between himself and Van Fleet. While acknowledging that he was fully informed regarding the dangerous situation that existed in the Koje compounds which were under Communist domination, he disclaims the possession of any accurate information on whatever corrective measures in progress, or under consideration, to alleviate these deplorable conditions. As Far

East Commander, it was his duty to be informed of such matters; and his evasive reply—"Every measure was taken, I *believe*, etc."—is tantamount to an admission of dereliction of duty.

The pattern of logic revealed in his further discussion of the reasons for maintaining the unhealthy concentration at Koje Island is little short of astonishing. If Ridgway honestly believed that breaking up the mammouth Koje compounds into smaller units of a size that were manageable imposed a critical drain on UN combat strength, where was the wisdom of postponing this disagreeable, but necessary, decision? The longer this crucial step was deferred, the more critical the situation at Koje-do was bound to become—if for no other reason than the fact that the POW population was constantly increasing.

It seems apparent that Van Fleet's acquiescence in this unfavorable situation was dictated by the belief that a truce settlement—which would have resolved the POW problem without the necessity for any further action on his part—was closer than it actually was. This is brought out by Ridgway's answers to Senator Saltonstall's queries in the following exchange:

"SENATOR SALTONSTALL: General Ridgway, I would like to ask you two questions on the Koje Island business, and then two other questions.

"As I listened to you on the problems with relation to the Koje Island situation, it seemed to me that it might be a plan on the part of the Communists to divert enough of our troops down there through the use of these prisoners to make us less effective up in the lines. Do you think it is a combined effort, a coordinated effort along these lines?

"GENERAL RIDGWAY: I think that is very possible. There certainly is a reasonable thesis, in my opinion, Senator Saltonstall. Everything these people do all ties into one over-all plan, and there is unquestionably an underground grapevine communication between those prisoner-of-war camps and the Communist headquarters.

[Statement deleted for security reasons]

"SENATOR SALTONSTALL: We are using a considerable number of United States Troops for POW guards are we not?

GENERAL RIDGWAY: Yes, sir.

[Statement deleted for security reasons]

"SENATOR SALTONSTALL: If that is so, why would it not be practical or is it practical to take some of those worst, the hard core prisoners, and move them further away, move them to Okinawa, for instance, where we are in good position?

"GENERAL RIDGWAY: We did the opposite, sir; so far we have done the opposite. We have left the hard core people all there in Koje-do, and we moved out the ones we thought were the most reliable, starting with the most friendly, those Communists whom we had screened, for instance, and who gave unmistakable evidence, in our opinion, that they would forcibly resist repatriation, and those we sent to the mainland because we considered them less of a risk in guarding, and would reduce the amount of additional overhead we would provide for their custody.

"SENATOR SALTONSTALL: So, you have sent them nearer rather than farther away. My idea was to make communication harder, and make it more difficult.

"GENERAL RIDGWAY: The ones we sent nearer were the ones that would give us and have given us the least trouble.

"SENATOR SALTONSTALL: But you have not sent the hardboiled ones any further away than Koje?

"GENERAL RIDGWAY: Yes, sir.

"SENATOR SALTONSTALL: Why would it not be good judgment to do that, sir?

"GENERAL RIDGWAY: We canvassed that, and we even considered sending them down to the Marianas or Saipan. But when you get to moving 50,000 or 60,000 people it is quite a problem with shipping and logistics support, and *we always had had the hope this would be concluded by an armistice in the near future, and we would not have to do that.* [Italics mine]

"Might I say, sir, that I even considered sending them back to the United States. Of course, it would have required approval from here, to get them out of this area, where they were such a potential danger.

"SENATOR SALTONSTALL: Well, listening to you this morning it would appear to me that that was the thing, perhaps, that we would have to do.

"GENERAL RIDGWAY: Yes, sir."

In the event, negotiations at Panmunjom dragged on for more than a year after the Dodd incident before an armistice was finally signed. Long before that, however, General Clark was compelled to take the measures which Van Fleet and Ridgway had done their best to avoid: namely, break up the oversize Koje-do compounds.

Throughout the whole period of Communist-instigated riots—and this period did not end, by any means, with the signing of concessions by General Colson—the truce proceedings cast a long shadow over operations at Koje Island. United Nations Command policies toward POW's were framed with one eye on military security and the other on Nam Il and his associates. There was, of course, the all-important matter of possible Communist reprisals against our own men held prisoner in Red camps. Senator Morse helped place this matter in perspective with his questions on press charges that the UNC had "coddled" Communist prisoners.

"CHAIRMAN RUSSELL: Senator Morse?

"SENATOR MORSE: I have one question on the prison matter, and then several on the over-all Korean problem.

"General, what liberty have we given the prisoners on Koje Island in excess of what we would be required to uhder the Geneva Convention?

"GENERAL RIDGWAY: None that I know of, Senator.

"SENATOR MORSE: We are limiting their liberties and their prerogatives to the Geneva Convention?

"GENERAL RIDGWAY: I believe so, scrupulously.

SENATOR MORSE: I am glad to hear that, because one would judge from the newspaper comments that apparently we have been soft on these prisoners.

"GENERAL RIDGWAY: I do not think so, sir. We have a fine type of American commander in control in an extremely difficult position. I want to emphasize that again, gentlemen. The question becomes a question of judgment down there as to whether in the face of this extreme provocation you are still going to use the force which results in killing a lot of people; and the cutting off of food and water to which Senator Russell referred, has been done repeatedly; whether it was done sufficiently or not I do not know. It is in the judgment of those local commanders.

[Statement deleted for security reasons]

"SENATOR MORSE: I suppose that in the treatment of these communist prisoners, we are probably influenced somewhat by a concern as to what would happen to our American prisoners if we used treatment that sometimes we think they ought to get of a more harsh nature?

"GENERAL RIDGWAY: They have intimated that directly during the course of the negotiations at Panmunjom. It is a veiled threat.

"SENATOR MORSE: Typical Communist blackmail.

"GENERAL RIDGWAY: Yes, typical Communist intimidation."

Lyndon B. Johnson, who at that time was a U.S. Senator from Texas, managed to get an important item introduced into the record when he elicited from General Ridgway a statement of the organizational set-up of the UNC prisoner of war command.

"SENATOR JOHNSON: General Ridgway, give the committee the chain of command from the Koje Island camp up to the top commander in Korea.

"GENERAL RIDGWAY: The camp commander who is appointed, to the commanding general, Second Logistical Command, who is General Yount, who is in Pusan, and he, in turn, is directly subordinate to General Van Fleet, commanding the Eighth Army.

"SENATOR JOHNSON: Who, in that chain of command, had the specific duty and responsibility for checking on General Dodd's duties?

"GENERAL RIDGWAY: General Yount.

"SENATOR JOHNSON: Did General Yount at any time indicate dissatisfaction with the performance of General Dodd?

"GENERAL RIDGWAY: No, sir; unless there would have been a report made to General Van Fleet, I would not know about it.

"SENATOR JOHNSON: To your knowledge, did General Colson check with any higher authority before signing this statement, this agreement?

"GENERAL RIDGWAY: I do not know, sir."

The crucial portion of the hearing was conducted by Senator Harry F. Byrd of Virginia.

Senator Byrd's cross-examination of Ridgway is a model of searching scrutiny. His questions were penetrating, and were selected with obvious care and forethought. His line of inquiry was pursued with vigor and tenacity of purpose.

General Ridgway's replies, on the other hand, were cautious and overqualified to the point of sounding downright evasive. The whole exchange is important enough to warrant being quoted in full.

Senator Byrd asked a few preliminary questions on U.S. military strength at Koje Island at the time of Dodd's capture. At least part of Ridgway's reply was deleted for security reasons. But he did make of an armored force of 17 standard tanks and 5 flame-thrower tanks; and with regard to troop strength, "There was a regiment of American troops there...and then two more battalions were sent in later."

"SENATOR BYRD: Was the situation so bad there that these prisoners without weapons can prevent a division of troops from—

"GENERAL RIDGWAY [interrupting]: We did not have anything like a division, Senator Byrd, there sir, and the 170,000 fanatical prisoners, if they all elected to make a break at the same time, would just stamp down the barbed wire as though it were matchsticks and then they are in among you, and that was one of the potentialities they had at any time."

Now this is just a bit disingenuous on General Ridgway's part. Leaving aside the question of U.S. troop strength and how much real military muscle was available at Koje-do, Ridgway's use of the figure 170,000 is highly suspect. If General Ridgway had been apprized at all of the internal political developments that had taken place in the Koje compounds over a span of more than eight months, he certainly should have known that over 50% of the 170,000 prisoners behind Koje-do barbed wire were fanatical *anti-Communists* who were hardly likely to be found tramplihg down fences and assaulting UN personnel.

But apparently General Ridgway's arithmetic had equal powers of expansion and contraction: any increase in numbers he gave away to the Communists, he could just as easily subtract from U.S. troop totals—as witness his quick denial of Senator Byrd's suggestion above.

The record does not contain any mention of whether Senator Byrd registered surprise at this point; but a note of surprise seems almost evident in his following questions.

"SENATOR BYRD: There was no effort made then to rescue General Dodd?

GENERAL RIDGWAY: By force, you mean, sir?

"SENATOR BYRD: Yes.

"GENERAL RIDGWAY: No, sir; none.

"SENATOR BYRD: How long was he in captivity?

"GENERAL RIDGWAY: About 80 hours, sir.

"SENATOR BYRD: In the meantime, when did the negotiations start for his release?

"GENERAL RIDGWAY: I think they started the afternoon of his seizure.

"SENATOR BYRD: You said you heard some fragmentary radio announcements. Do you recall what you did here?

"GENERAL RIDGWAY: In what respect, sir?

"SENATOR BYRD: In regard to the demands made by the Communists.

"GENERAL RIDGWAY: I did not hear of the demands made except of a purely administrative nature. They wanted a lot of stationery and stuff in the first 24 hours, and I did not hear the other demands that they subsequently made, except in a general way.

"SENATOR BYRD: What is your understanding of the agreement that General—who is it—Colson, did you say?

"GENERAL RIDGWAY: General Colson made.

"SENATOR BYRD: In other words, what were they to do in return for the giving up of the person of General Dodd?

"GENERAL RIDGWAY: Well, that is what I have not seen in the official report, Senator.

"SENATOR BYRD: What is your understanding?
"GENERAL RIDGWAY: My understanding is that the demands made would have, no matter how you replied, involved a tacit admission of some of the allegations whech the Communists had made about inhumane treatment of prisoners of war, the use of germ warfare, and things of that sort.

It was sort of the type of question of "When did you stop beating your wife?" No matter what you answered, you were over a barrel, and it was for that reason, as I said, that on the afternoon of the 10th, Saturday afternoon, when I first heard that some demands were being made that I sent an immediate directive over there that no reply whatever would be made.

Another demand for release would be made but no reply would be made to their demands, and late that same afternoon, early Saturday evening, I found that some reply had already been made.
"SENATOR BYRD: But the actual deal between the two had not been consummated, had it?
"GENERAL RIDGWAY: Not at that time; no, sir.
"SENATOR BYRD: Why didn't you order them to stop that?
"GENERAL RIDGWAY: I do not quite follow you there, sir.
"SENATOR BYRD: You said that no reply would be made.
"GENERAL RIDGWAY: Yes, sir.
"SENATOR BYRD: Did you not?
"GENERAL RIDGWAY: Yes.
"SENATOR BYRD: Well, after a reply was made, why wouldn't it have been possible for you to give an order that General Dodd should not say that he thought that we were guilty of these acts?
"GENERAL RIDGWAY: Well, I did not know; I could not find out, Senator Byrd, exactly what reply had been made, and I had given a perfectly explicit and adequate directive to the Eighth Army, the

directive with which I opened my remarks here, that he would, without delay, bring about the release of General Dodd; that he was authorized and directed to use whatever force was necessary, and I did not want to get into the detailed conduct of those things from Tokyo, when I was not in possession of all the facts.

"My directive to him I considered then, and I still consider, completely adequate. He was ordered to use whatever force was necessary to accomplish this purpose.

"SENATOR BYRD: Your first directive was that no reply should be made?

"GENERAL RIDGWAY: No, sir; that was not in the first directive. My directive, as I just mentioned, sir, was within the first 24 hours; this other that no reply was to be made was Saturday afternoon, when I understood some demand had been made, the nature of which I was not informed of.

"SENATOR BYRD: Then, a reply was made?

"GENERAL RIDGWAY: A reply was made, sir.

"SENATOR BYRD: And other replies were made. This thing could not have been negotiated by just one transmission of messages?

"GENERAL RIDGWAY: That is right, sir.

"SENATOR BYRD: Why was it then that you did not issue an order that all negotiations stop as long as you—that you did not want any reply made, and one reply was made, and other replies were made, why not stop them after the first one?

"GENERAL RIDGWAY: That I left to General Van Fleet, sir. I told him what I wanted done in no unmistakable terms.

"SENATOR BYRD: Did the negotiations violate your directions, do you think, your directives?

"GENERAL RIDGWAY: I would not say they violated them directly, sir. There was a question of judgment, sir, as to whether they

produced the result without delay. I do not think they did.
"SENATOR BYRD: Your first directive, or one of your directives, was that no reply should be made of it; and it would seem to me to follow—
"GENERAL RIDGWAY: It had already been made, sir.
"SENATOR BYRD: I know, but then the negotiations had not been completed. If you did not want any reply made to them, and you started to negotiate, you could stop the negotiations, it seems to me.
"GENERAL RIDGWAY: Well, Senator Byrd, it is my recollection again—I must say, sir, that anything that I do not give you here is because of sheer lack of knowing the facts—it is my impression as follows: That my instructions that there would be no answer came too late. When I heard that there had been these demands, and directed there be no reply whatever, the reply had already been made. All the essential damage which may have occurred from those negotiations took place up to that time. Thereafter, there was, based on the knowledge I now have, in my opinion, no substantial damage to our interests.

"*The release of General Dodd, in my opinion, was produced by the rapidity with which the Communists saw the means being assembled there, and their analysis that the determination was present to go in and get General Dodd or to compel obedience.* [Italics mine]
"SENATOR BYRD: Now, the papers reported something about making a condition of screening the prisoners, and so forth. One of the conditions for the release of General Dodd was the screening. Do you know anything about that?
"GENERAL RIDGWAY: Yes, sir; I was able to see that the demands, one of the demands, was there would be no more screening. Obviously, General Colson, and no other person there, had any authority to agree to any such demand.

"SENATOR BYRD: Do you know whether General Colson agreed to that or not?

"GENERAL RIDGWAY: No, sir; I do not.

"SENATOR BYRD: Who is it that can give this committee and Congress the full and complete statement of what occurred?

"GENERAL RIDGWAY: I doubt if anybody here can until those fully documented reports arrive from Korea.

"SENATOR BYRD: Has General Clark made a report yet?

"GENERAL RIDGWAY: I do not think he has. He has made a report but I do not think it is here in Washington.

"SENATOR BYRD: Well, I am informed that the report has been received here, maybe my information is not correct.

"GENERAL RIDGWAY: Maybe that is correct.

"SENATOR JOHNSON: Secretary Pace reported to Senator Bridges and myself the night before last that he had a preliminary report, and he expected a full report from General Clark by Thursday of this week, is that right?

"SENATOR BRIDGES: Yes.

"GENERAL RIDGWAY: I think it is coming by courier; it is too voluminous to come by radio.

"SENATOR BYRD: When was the board—who comprises the board that was appointed?

"GENERAL RIDGWAY: That I do not know either, sir. It was appointed after my departure. I think there were two boards, Senator Byrd; one appointed by General Van Fleet, which made the immediate investigation, and another board, I understand, appointed by General Clark from his own staff, an independent investigation.

"SENATOR BYRD: Do you see any objection to the publication to the public of the preliminary report of General Clark, so far as you are advised?

"GENERAL RIDGWAY: Well, it would be beyond my purview, and I have not seen its contents; I do not know what is in it.

"SENATOR BYRD: That is all, Mr. Chairman."

Matthew B. Ridgway is one of the most pugnacious officers who ever wore the uniform of the U.S. Army. Anyone who is at all familiar with his characteristically blunt, forthright, soldierly utterances might be hard put to identify him in the preceding exchange. His cautious, overqualified, and evasive replies to Senator Byrd's pointed questions are decidedly atypical of Ridgway, and lead an impartial observer to agree with the news correspondent who summarized the aftermath of the Dodd incident as "a fast game of buck-passing among the generals."

And, as an old soldier, General Ridgway knows that the buck is never passed *up*.

CHAPTER TEN

Operation Breakup

Our feelings we with difficulty smother—
When constabulary duty's to be done—
Ah, take one consideration with another—
A policeman's lot is not a happy one.
GILBERT & SULLIVAN: *Pirates of Penzance*

ON JUNE 10, 1952, one month and three days after the horse had been stolen, the United Nations Command made arrangements to bolt the barn door. By the time the latch was finally secured, it turned out to be a rather involved and costly operation. Chief Locksmith was a new Koje-do commander—the 14th in less than two years—who added a dash of bright color to the otherwise drab Korean war: "Buster" Boatner.[1]

Brigadier General Haydon L. Boatner came to Koje Island from the 2nd Infantry Division ("Second to None!" as their motto would have it) where he had been serving as deputy division commander. Tough, cocky, self-reliant, and highly competent, General Boatner brought with him to his new command an outstanding combat record in two world wars and a couple of unorthodox, but exceedingly valuable, personal qualifications.

For one thing, he was a fluent Chinese linguist. In any future parleys with recalcitrant Chinese prisoners, General Boatner could dispense with the offices of an interpreter.

For another, he possessed a thorough first-hand knowledge of China and the Chinese. Under General Boatner there would be no repetition of mishaps like that of the red POW uniforms—an incident which arose from sheer ignorance on the part of the camp commander and his staff of the psychology of their Korean prisoners.

After World War I, in which he had enlisted as a private in the Marine Corps at the ripe old age of 18, Boatner entered West Point. During succeeding years, he saw long service in China; and in World War II, Boatner was Chief of Staff to crusty General "Vinegar Joe" Stillwell. In the China-Burma-India theater, Boatner acquired a reputation as a hard-driving, aggressive officer who was fearlessly outspoken. In the Korean war, he fought with the Second Division at Heartbreak Ridge, one of the bloodiest actions of the whole campaign.

From the bleak vantage point of command, Koje-do's grim compounds must have seemed like Heartbreak Ridge all over again.

"This amazing, unbelievable situation," wrote General Clark, "in which the POW's controlled their compounds, did not end with the release of Dodd. On the contrary, it was strengthened if anything by the demonstration of rebellious power and by the concessions signed by Colson." Nothing had changed. American guards were still staying outside of Communist enclosures. The POW's were still flying their tauntingly offensive signs and banners. The Communist ringleaders from other compounds who had been admitted to Compound 76, the stockade where the Dodd kidnapping had taken place, were still there and refused to leave. If General Boatner proved capable of rectifying this situation without further violence and bloodshed, he would show himself as something more than an exceptional officer—a veritable Houdini in OG's.

On assuming command of UN POW Camp 1, General Boatner told the press that he intended to establish control over conditions within the compounds, put an immediate halt to the flaunting of Red flags and insulting signs, and squelch any further attempts by the Communists to serve demands on the camp authorities. "Prisoners of war do not negotiate," he declared emphatically. He promised the Reds humane treatment, but pointed out that they had always been treated with greater leniency than required by the rules of civilized warfare or the terms of the Geneva Convention.

A few days later, on May 20th, trouble flared anew in UN Prison Camp 10 at Pusan, when guards broke up a sitdown strike staged by Red prisoners in the camp hospital. The demonstrators were non-patient workers and orderlies who resisted commands to leave the hospital. They fought the guards with makeshift weapons. One Communist prisoner was killed and 85 POW's were injured. An American guard was wounded slightly in this outbreak. On May 22nd, the U.S. Army issued a statement that the disorder had been quelled and that a program was underway to segregate troublemakers in the Pusan camp.

Boatner's campaign to win uncontested control of the Koje Island compounds got started on June 1st, when he ordered the Red leader of Compound 66, a North Korean lieutenant colonel, placed in special confinement and sent troops and tanks into Compounds 60, 85, 96, and 607. Red flag poles were torn down. Compound 607 was fenced into two units, and rebellious Communist prisoners in Compounds 85 and 96 were put on short rations. One day earlier, 5 Reds were killed while trying to pass messages between compounds.

On June 2nd, General Mark Clark paid an official visit to Koje-do. The United Nations Supreme Commander gave full indorsement to General Boatner's program. He stated that the UNC was prepared to use maximum force in order to establish and maintain control over mutinous Communist prisoners.

Following Clark's visit, security measures were tightened still further at Koje. General Boatner ordered all civilian residents off the island, put through a complete reorganization of the POW camp command, and directed the construction of new compounds designed to hold from 500 to 1,000 men. The UN Command had finally conceded the wisdom of breaking up the huge, unwieldy Koje compounds into smaller, more manageable units. To assist the camp garrison in carrying out the transfer of prisoners to the new stockades, combat-seasoned paratroopers of the 187th Regimental Combat Team, under the command of Brigadier General Thomas Trapnell, were dispatched to Koje Island.

"Staff planning for this operation," said General Clark, "was done as carefully as for any orthodox military campaign. We knew by this time that the Communist POW's were active combatants and had to be dealt with as soldiers, not prisoners in the traditional sense." That the Communist prisoners had made their own comprehensive staff preparations for the impending transfer operation shortly became evident. Their military plans were foiled, however, by the staunch determination and resolute action of General Boatner and his men.

On June 10, 1952, exactly one month after the release of General Dodd, Boatner moved in on the toughest of the compounds: Number 76. The Communists were spoiling for a fight. For the past month there had been a series of skirmishes with the United Nations guards in celebration of their "victory" at Koje-do. They were fully prepared to resist any attempts at removal of the POW's. They had armed themselves with the usual assortment of crude weapons—barbed wire flails, clubs, hatchets, pikes—and had manufactured Molotov cocktails from hoarded cooking gasoline. Before the main gate of the compound some of the prisoners had dug a waist-deep slit-trench, expecting that the guards would try to force an entrance there.

At 5: 45 a.m. public address loudspeakers in Compound 76 broadcast a message to the prisoners that they were to be moved into new quarters that day. They were told that no punitive action would be taken against them if they cooperated with the camp authorities.

The broadcast was a waste of time.

Communist prisoners cut loose with a barrage of invective aimed at the UN guards. They pointedly ignored Boatner's order to form into groups of 150 in preparation for the movement. Instead, they openly armed themselves with spears made from sharpened tent poles, knives, clubs, and rocks. They chanted their defiance and shouted insults at the American troops as their leaders whipped them into a fighting frenzy.

At 6:15 a.m. half an hour after the messages to the POW's had begun, 1,000 men of the 187th RCT closed in for a showdown. They made no attempt to breach the heavily-fortified front gate. While medium tanks patrolled the perimeter of the stockade, combat engineers cut through the barbed wire at the rear of the enclosure.

Boatner knew that the Communist High Command made the fullest propaganda use of Red "martyrs" in the POW camps. Accordingly, he did everything he could to avoid casualties. He ordered his men to attack with tear gas and concussion grenades only. They followed his orders unswervingly and brought the Red demonstrators under control without firing a single shot.

The tough paratroopers relied entirely on riot tactics. Wearing gas masks, the troops of the 187th RCT advanced through cuts in the barbed wire and lobbed tear gas grenades into the surging mob. The grenades ignited stores of gasoline that the Communists had secreted in the compound, whereupon the POW's broke and scattered before the American advance. Some ducked into the barracks and locked the doors; others jumped into the ditch near the main gate.

Our troops began a methodical job of hustling the Reds out of the barracks and the slit-trenches, herding the prisoners toward the center of the compound. In an hour and a half, the fight was over. "Most of the prisoners permitted themselves to be evacuated without difficulty," General Clark declared, "but the last fifteen hundred of the six thousand POW's of the compound formed ranks in a moblike group in one corner. They resisted with stubborn fanaticism as the UN soldiers tried to break them up into smaller groups."

Nevertheless, by 8:45 a. m. six thousand North Koreans squatted on their heels in the assembly area while the compound's buildings went up in flames. Shortly afterward the prisoners were moved to the new compounds. Their leaders were led off to solitary confinement.

It had been a bloody piece of business. One American soldier was dead and fourteen others were wounded. The Communists had lost thirty-one dead and 139 wounded.

During the hottest part of the action, prisoners had been seen fighting among themselves. At least a dozen POW's were killed by other prisoners, to prevent them from surrendering to the American paratroopers. The Communist leaders had fought not only to hold off the U. S. Army, but also to avert a mass defection among their own men. After the compound was cleared of prisoners, a search and examination revealed shocking conditions. According to General Clark:

> "The prisoners had fashioned about 3,000 spears from tent poles, 1,000 gasoline grenades, 4,500 knives and an uncounted number of clubs, hatchets, hammers and barbed wire flails. A tunnel was under construction from Compound 76 to Compound 77. Trenches surrounded each hut and connected one building to another in a network that covered the compound.

"The battle in Compound 76 yielded some of the top Communist leaders in the camp, including Colonel Lee Hak Koo...Lee and other compound leaders were segregated, but there were others to take their places later.

"In addition to the weapons and entrenchments found in Compound 76, our troops discovered a document detailing a complete plan of battle for the resistance to the breakup operation. The well-disciplined prisoners had followed the plan almost to the letter in their fight against Boatner's troops."

General Boatner's decisive handling of Compound 76 promptly wilted resistance in other enclosures. Six thousand prisoners in Compound 78 and another six thousand from Compound 77 were marched to new compounds without any difficulty, When the 4,800 inmates of Compound 95 were moved out on June 12th, about 500 anti-Red POW's bolted and asked the camp authorities for protection.

The leader of the Red officer POW's in Compound 66 was shown battlewrecked Compound 76 as an object lesson, after this group had shown a readiness to resist removal. They also abandoned the struggle.

Another focal source of disturbance was eliminated. Boatner moved the Korean village which had long functioned as a nerve center in the communications network established by Nam Il's agents. Controls were tightened to make contact between the prisoners and the Korean townspeople virtually impossible.

General Boatner instituted other precautionary measures. Said Clark: "Compound inspections by camp authorities, impossible in some of the enclosures in the past, were made daily in every compound. The POW's were no longer able to declare any part of the camps off limits to UN troops. There were regular searches for contraband to prevent any repetition of the astonishing build-up of an arsenal by the POW's...Intelligence systems were expanded to give more complete information about what was going on inside the compounds and especially to identify and segregate the men who were leaders in Nam Il's organization. The hospital setup was revised so that no longer did the prisoners have such a convenient message center for their communications network. And effective steps were taken to catch the Nam Il agents who permitted themselves to be captured so they could carry messages and directives into the prison compounds. The safeguards were simple. I directed that newly captured POW's be kept in new compounds, apart from old prisoners."

In the short space of ten days, General Boatner had moved over 70,000 prisoners to the new compounds and had segregated the anti-Communists from those who were willing to accept repatriation to North Korea or China. Finally, on June 19th, about 1,000 Red civilian internees in Compound 62 were transferred to a new stockade.

"Operation Breakup" was officially over.

You cannot make an omelette, William L. White observed, without breaking eggs. It was just about this time that the United Nations Command found itself in receipt of some strongly-worded protests from the International Red Cross. Since the 7th of May—the date of General Dodd's capture by the prisoners of Compound 76—the UNC had been compelled to bar the IRC representatives from Koje and other mutinous compounds where their safety could not be guaranteed. This ban continued until the early part of July.

"In mid-May," said White, "Delegate Lehner, head of the IRC mission, made a visit to Tokyo to take up with Commanding General Mark Clark not only this ban, but other matters. For when prisoners in Enclosure 10 had refused to leave for their newer and smaller pens, we had cut off food and water to make them leave. In a stern letter to Mark Clark, Delegate Lehner insisted this was an infringement of

Article 26 of the Geneva Convention, which states that 'collective disciplinary measures affecting food are prohibited.'"

Lehner also objected that UN troops had used concussion grenades against the Red prisoners, which had "caused at least one death and several wounded. He requested that General Clark issue orders to the UNC "to refrain in the future from coercive measures of the abovementioned kind."

"Why this rebuke?" asks White. "Perhaps we deserved it. Or perhaps the International Red Cross, goaded by Communist attacks on them for lack of neutrality, felt that severe censure of U.N. conduct might be helpful at this time."

At any rate, General Clark waited until the Koje mess was straightened out before replying to the International Red Cross. According to White:

"...in a blistering letter to Dr. Lehner, he reminded him that, 'as you are fully aware', this compound 'controlled by fanatical Communist leaders' had excluded everyone, barring even 'peaceable entry of our medical personnel' needed to help the sick.

"He reminded the IRC that 'your delegates...witnessed the prisoners' disregard of lawful orders' and themselves 'attempted for several days to secure the cooperation of the prisoners but were unsuccessful', after which 'these same delegates, as well as yourself, agreed that uncontested control had to be established, but could offer no satisfactory method by which this could be accomplished'.

"Was our method too harsh? "Food and water were made available in the new compound, and the rebellious prisoners informed that rations would no longer be delivered to the three compounds they occupied.' So 'at no time were the prisoners denied them'.

"As for the rough treatment, 'carefully trained United States troops, fully oriented on the necessity of keeping violence to an absolute minimum' had moved against the 'aggressive prisoners armed with a variety of lethal weapons which they had fashioned' and our troops had used only tear gas and a concussion grenade of the shock type, which 'is not considered a combat missile'.

"Then General Clark, 'while fully recognizing your right to state your views', insisted that 'your report should include a resumé of the circumstances that led to the action at Pusan—circumstances which are fully known to you' and asked that 'this communication be forwarded to your headquarters with whatever official report you may make'."

Nothing more was heard from the International Red Cross thereafter about the UNC's "coercive measures."

"Right after the Koje incident," said Clark, "I had requested the authority to bring to trial all of the ringleaders responsible for crimes in the prison camps." Most prominent in this category were the members of the "General Leading Headquarters" of the Communist political organization within the prison camp. Colonel Lee Hak Koo and "Private" Pak Sang Hyong were taken out of the compound and held separately.

"Are you trying to prove that the USSR is running the Korean war?" Pak asked. "That is not necessary. I am living proof of that fact." Pak asked for a Russian-speaking interpreter because he was—he said proudly—a Soviet citizen of Korean extraction and an officer in the Red Army.

Shortly afterward Pak decided to come over to the UN side. Since his revolt had failed, he was anxious to reject repatriation. He knew that he would receive short shrift back in North Korea. He now related the whole story of his POW organization, its methodical plans and procedures, and its central direction by General Nam Il at Panmunjom.

Washington had stalled on General Clark's request to try the Communist criminals, ostensibly for fear that the trials might compromise the chances of a cease-fire agreement. However, Clark said, "as additional crimes were committed and Allied personnel were killed or wounded, I repeated my request for authority to bring these criminals to justice as the only means of enforcing discipline. I also pointed out that under the Geneva Convention we had the responsibility to safeguard the prisoners in our control and that we failed to fulfill this obligation when we failed to halt the kangaroo courts which ordered anti-Communist prisoners to be beaten to death. Finally I was given authority to try these Communist criminals for postcapture offenses. I had prisoners who were known to have committed atrocities against American and other Allied troops before they were captured, but I was not given authority to try these men."

As the truce negotiations appeared to be nearing a long-awaited resolution, Clark was engaged in setting up a UN tribunal to try criminal offenses committed in the prison camps. However, when he asked the authorities in Washington whether he was to hold the prisoners in "Operation Big Switch"—the POW exchange—he was ordered to hand them over to the Communists. This decision, General Clark stated, "was based on fear that if we held back some of these prominent Communist leaders, who had served their masters so well in the military campaign in the POW camps, then the enemy would retaliate by retaining Major General William F. Dean and other senior UN prisoners still in their hands."

Pak Sang Hyong turned his coat once more. After the signing of the armistice, Pak was repatriated to North Korea, along with the other Communist ringleaders who had perpetrated crimes against both UN guard personnel and their fellow captives. It can only be assumed that they are now profitably employed in their Communist homelands disseminating the conclusions of their sojourn among the fatuous Americans and preparing plans for future Koje-type operations in prison compounds of the future.

So much for American indulgence and naïvete.

CHAPTER ELEVEN

Sequel at Cheju-do & Pongam

AFTER HE HAD SUBDUED the unruly Communist prisoners at Koje-do and restored some tranquillity to the camp, General Boatner continued with "Operation Breakup." Off to the Korean mainland went 48,000 anti-Communist Koreans, to be detained in six widely dispersed camps. The hard-core Communist north Koreans were left on Koje, and on neighboring Choju and Pongam islands. All 20,000 Chinese POW's were shipped off to the large, mountainous island of Cheju, off the southwestern coast of Korea.

But General Boatner's headaches did not end with the successful completion of "Operation Breakup."

The first indication that Communist agents had infiltrated the anti-Communist camps came from an investigation of disturbances at United Nations POW Camp 16 at Nonsan. According to General Clark:

> "Anti-Communist prisoners charged that a group of North Koreans had been shipped from Koje-do posing as anti-Communists in order to penetrate mainland camps and create unrest and violence. The anti-Communist prisoners charged these alleged agents planned to assassinate anti-Communist leaders and take control of entire compounds in much the same manner as their predecessors on Koje."

But this time the anti-Communist prisoners turned the tables. Using the tactics of the Communists, they seized the agitators, grilled them, and tried to beat them into making confessions of planned resistance. They did such a thorough job that one Red prisoner died from the beating and seven others ended up in the camp hospital.

Several days later, 24 more North Koreans were injured in a similar incident. Investigation disclosed that there were definitely Communist agents in the camp and that they were fighting to wrest power from the anti-Communists. But the latter had taken the lessons of Koje-do to heart. They were organized and ready to cope with Communist attempts at subversion.

Meanwhile, on Cheju-do, there were signs of an impending disturbance.

Some 14,000 Chinese who had rejected Communism were penned up at one end of the island, and 5,800 loyal Reds—every one of them a constant troublemaker—were held at the other end.

General Boatner had been given another star for his effective handling of the difficult Koje situation. With the new title of Deputy Commander of the 2nd Logistical Command for Prisoner-of-War Affairs, his authority extended to all United Nations POW camps in Korea. Unfortunately, he was rotated to the United States at the end of the summer—just as his skills and firm guidance were needed most desperately.

"Behind him," read a press eulogy, "he left the doctrine that the way to treat Communists is to tread carefully the narrow line between too much severity and too much laxity. In cases of defiance, non-fatal weapons such as tear gas, concussion grenades, rifle butts and shotguns (firing small shot) were to be preferred to bullets. Prisoners should be allowed to celebrate Red holidays if they were orderly and obeyed the rules."

Boatner had been gone a little over a month when the Communist Chinese on Cheju-do filed notice of their desire to celebrate the third anniversary of the Chinese "People's Republic." By an ill-timed coincidence, the camp commander was stricken with a heart ailment, and a new officer—an infantry colonel named Richard Boerem—had been sent to replace him. By a further unfortunate coincidence, the older contingent of guards had been replaced by a battalion of U. S. Army troops fresh from combat.

Colonel Boerem, it soon turned out, had ideas of his own on the subject of Communist holidays. He curtly refused to allow the Red Chinese prisoners at Cheju-do to celebrate the "People's Republic" anniversary in any manner.

On the big day, the inmates of Compound 7 broke out illegal Communist flags and hoisted them on makeshift poles. When the colonel sent in a detail of guards to take down the flags, they were met with a shower of stones. Reinforcements were rushed to their aid, but the barrage increased.

Then, according to one correspondent's account, "a U. S. officer, whose wife and child had been killed by the Communists in China, raised his pistol and shot one Chinese. The other Americans regarded his shot as a signal and began firing. Once inside the compound they were set upon by prisoners wielding clubs, sharpened tent poles and barbed wire flails, but these attackers were shot down before they could close. Fifteen minutes after it started, the battle was over. Fifty-six Chinese were dead or dying, 100 others wounded. Two Americans were wounded. Already, Haydon L. Boatner was being sadly missed."

A few weeks later, he was even more sorely missed at Pongam.

This camp housed civilian pro-Communists who had been moved out of Koje. Said General Clark, "There had been a series of small disturbances all month. On December 4th POWs in one compound refused to show their clothing and equipment for inspection. Two days later camp authorities at Koje said they had uncovered evidence which indicated that prisoners in the main camp and its branches, which included Pongam, might be planning a mass escape. Next day prisoners at Pongam defied camp authorities and conducted military drills in three compounds. Three days later, on the tenth, a small group of Pongam prisoners attacked an administrative soldier at a dispensary enclosure and next day two prisoners attacked an enclosure commander."

This gradual build-up of defiance exploded with a roar on December 14th in six compounds of Pongam's Enclosure 2 where 3,600 of the camp's 9,000 prisoners were quartered.

The riot began when the POW's in each of the six compounds massed together in a close-knit and obviously well-planned military drill in defiance of camp rules. The prisoners formed ranks at the top of a high terrace; and when guards at the foot of the steep incline ordered them to disperse, they responded with a hail of stones. A stiff breeze cancelled the effective use of tear gas, and a warning volley of shots had no effect. Three waves of taunting and jeering prisoners, with arms locked together, bore down relentlessly on the guards. Lieutenant Colonel George Miller, the island commander, instructed his men to lower the muzzles of their rifles and fire. In the brief battle that followed, 82 prisoners were killed and 120 were wounded—the highest casualty rate ever recorded in any Korean POW riot.

The Communists, said General Clark, "seized upon this incident immediately. A letter was circulated among Party members inside the compounds exhorting them to emulate the example of the 'heroes' who died at Pongam. Object: force the Americans to kill more prisoners so that 'throughout the world' the Yankee will be known as 'the enemy of human beings.'"

Six months still remained before the signing of the truce at Panmunjom. While there were no further disturbances on the scale of the

Pongam riot, the Communists continued to the bitter end to foment violence and bloodshed. "That is a case history of our enemy wherever he may be found," General Clark stated. An enemy who is "resourceful, imaginative, fanatic, dangerous."

It is the same enemy we face today.

CHAPTER TWELVE

Not with a Bang but a Whimper

AT 10 O'CLOCK ON THE MORNING OF JULY 27, 1953—after 747 days, 575 regular meetings, and 18,000,000 words of acrimonious debate—the Korean Armistice Agreeement was signed in Panmunjom. The document bore the signatures of General Nam Il, senior Red delegate to the truce proceedings, and General William K. Harrison USA, chief representative for the United Nations. Later that day, the guns were silenced all along the battlefront. Troops of both sides, by prearranged plan, fell back behind a two and a half mile buffer strip—the DMZ or Demilitarized Zone—which separated the Republic of Korea from the Communist state to the north. The war in Korea was finally over, following the most protracted armistice negotiations in history—a "merry-go-round talkathon," as some correspondent called it.

After the swoon, the syntax...

Hardly had the roar of battle died away into silence when the debates began again, this time on the same side of the conference table. Like most compromises, the Korean armistice pleased nobody and offended everybody. And one of the chief targets for critical comment was the issue over which the Communists had staged the bloody riots at Koje-do and which they had bitterly resisted for two years and seventeen days: voluntary repatriation.

Eisenhower, whom no one accused of special pleading, took a sanguinary view. In a speech given at Columbia University, he said: "The armistice in Korea has inaugurated a new principle of freedom —that prisoners of war are entitled to choose the side to which they will be released. In its impact on history, that one principle may weigh more than any battle of our time."

The chief architect of the Armistice Agreement, Vice Admiral C. Turner Joy, held a sharply differing opinion: "Voluntary repatriation cost us over a year of war, and cost our United Nations Command prisoners in Communist camps a year of captivity. The United Nations Command suffered at least 50,000 casualties in the continuing Korean War while we argued to protect a lesser number of ex-Communists who did not wish to return to Communism."

One of the main objectives in holding out for the principle of "no forced repatriation" was the belief—or rather the fond hope—that the prospect of political asylum would prove an effective psychological weapon against the Communist regime. "I regret to say," Admiral Joy commented, "this does not seem to have been a valid point. There have been no wholesale defections from Asiatic Communism flowing from *our* demonstration that asylum would be granted. Nor has our demonstration deterred the Communists from their aggression in Indochina and their present warlike intentions point to Formosa. Whatever temporary loss of prestige in Asia Communism suffered from the results of 'voluntary repatriation' has long since been overtaken by Communism's subsequent victory in that area."

Communist motives in blocking the exchange of prisoners had been a matter for speculation throughout the long, wearisome negotiations. Said Rutherford Poats:

> "The Communists'... stubborn refusal to compromise on their demand that every Red captive be repatriated, at bayonet point if necessary, suggested to many officials and observers that delay was

the Reds' objective. According to this theory, the prisoner-exchange controversy merely provided the most plausible excuse for delay; it was argued that, if the United Nations Command had not raised the voluntary repatriation issue, the Communists would have found another issue on which to block an armistice. Such speculation is fruitless, because even in retrospect we lack real knowledge of the decisions taken in Communist secret councils.

"Only this much is clear: for eighteen months neither side so desperately wanted a truce, or so clearly saw the way to converting the armistice into a peace favorable to its own interests, as to be willing to compromise after the prisoner-exchange deadlock developed. Later, too much 'face' was involved; the repatriation issue had become a symbol."

Which raises an important question: Why did the Communists finally accept the principle of voluntary repatriation after so much resistance?

Admiral Joy has an answer, but it is one that will offer little comfort to those who feel that negotiation with the Communists is the solution to the problems of coexistence in a world rent by opposing ideologies:

"Since they had capitalized on the armistice conference by preparing and occupying almost impregnable defense positions, the desultory war in Korea was not too much for them to bear. Nor is it useful to look to the area of reason and logic for the answer. No, I think the cause of Communist acquiescence in the principle of voluntry repatriation was neither the continuing hostilities in Korea nor the mercurial status of world opinion. Their plans for the conquest of Indochina may have influenced their ultimate decision. But what influenced them most, I feel certain, were ominous sounds of impending *expanded* warfare, the prospect of United Nations

Command forces being released from their confinement to Korea and allowed to range over Red China. During the spring of 1953, the United States began running out of patience. Serious consideration was being given to extending United Nations Command military operations into Red China. The threat of atom bombs was posed: defeat for Red China became a distinct possibility. Thus at the last, the one negotiating factor that Communists respect above all else was beginning to appear: naked, massive power and the willingness to use that power when necessary. Red China did not dare to challenge the unrestrained military might of the United States. That way lay ruin. In understandable prudence, they took the only step open to them to remove the growing threat of a holocaust in Red China. It was as simple as that. It had always been as simple as that."

During the interminable and exhausting arguments over the exchange of POW's, Admiral Joy charged, the Communists "engaged in every nefarious practice known to them. They lied; they blustered; they became vindictive; they welshed; they twisted, distorted, and denied truth; they delayed; they threatened." If Communist actions at Panmunjom were at all consistent with Communist motives, the achievement of a just and equitable cease-fire arrangement was the last of their intentions—as Admiral Joy declared in the blunt language of his concluding address to the members of the Red delegation:

"It has become increasingly clear through these long-drawn-out conferences that any hope that your side would bring good faith to these meetings was forlorn indeed. From the very start, you have caviled over procedural details; you have manufactured spurious issues and placed them in controversy for bargaining purposes; you have denied the existence of agreements made between us when you found the fulfillment thereof not to your liking; you have indulged in abuse and invective when all other tactics proved ineffective. Through a constant succession of delays, fraudulent arguments, and artificial attitudes you have obstructed the attainment of an armistice which easily lay within our grasp had there been equal honesty on both sides of this conference table. Nowhere in the record is there a single action of your side which indicates a real and sincere desire to attain the objective for which these conferences were designed. Instead, you have increasingly presented evidence before the world that you did not enter these negotiations with sincerity and high purpose, but rather that you entered into them to gain time to repair your shattered forces and to try to accomplish at the conference table what your armies could not accomplish in the field. It is an enormous misfortune that you are constitutionally incapable of understanding the fair and dignified attitude of the United Nations Command. Apparently you cannot comprehend that strong and proud and free nations can make costly sacrifices for principles because they are strong; can be dignified in the face of abuse and deceit because they are proud, and can speak honestly because they are free and do not fear the truth. Instead, you impute to the United Nations Command the same suspicion, greed, and deviousness which are your stock in trade. You search every word for a hidden meaning and every agreement for a hidden trap. It would be charitable for me to say that you do these things by instinct, but you are people of intelligence and it is probably truer to say that you do these things with purpose and design.

"From the very first, the United Nations Command has had but one objective in Korea: To bring an end to the Korean war so that a permanent and enduring peace might be established as quickly as possible. This has been the precise objective of the United Nations Command delegation in these negotiations. This is what we meant by good faith on our part. You have but to examine the record to see the many evidences of our restraint, our constructive suggestions, our willingness to conciliate and compromise, and our patience. There is very little evidencc of similar contributions by your side. As an answer to the question, "Which side has brought good faith to these meetings?" nothing could be more impressive than a comparison of the actions of the two delegations during our ten months of these conferences. They are as different as night and day. No amount of propaganda, however oft repeated, can hide your ignoble record. That these meetings have continued this long and that we have, after a fashion, resolved our differences to the point where only one major issue remains is testimony to the patience and dedication of the United Nations Command.

"Now our negotiations have come to the point where the prisoner-of-war issue stands as a formidable barrier to the accomplishment of an armistice. Casting aside any pretense of humanity, you have made the demand that the United Nations Command must return to your side all the prisoners of war in its custody, driving them at the point of a bayonet if necessary. You even have the colossal impertinence to document your position by referring to the Geneva Convention. What could be more ironic than your attempt to found your inhuman proposition upon an international agreement whose purpose is to defend and protect the unfortunate victims of war? You who have denied the International Red Cross access to your prisoner-of-war camps, who have refused to furnish lists of prisoners to the Prisoner of War Bureau, and who cannot even account for over fifty thousand (50,000) United Nations Command soldiers whom you officially boasted as having in your custody before the Korean war was nine months old. After months of conciliation, of meeting you more than halfway on issue after issue, the United

Nations Command has told you with full firmness and finality that it will not recede from its position with respect to the prisoners of war. On the 28th of April we offered you an equitable and specific solution to the issues remaining before us. We told you then, and we repeat now, that we firmly adhere to the principles of humanity and the preservation of the rights of the individual. These are values which we will not barter, for they are one and the same with the principles which motivated the United Nations Command to oppose you on the battlefield. No amount of argument and invective will move us. If you harbor the slightest desire to restore peace and to end the misery and suffering of millions of innocent people, you must bring to the solution of this issue the good faith which, as I said at our first meeting, would directly determine the success or failure of our negotiations. The decision is in your hands."

No American can read the transcripts of these proceedings at Panmunjom without a deep feeling of respect and admiration for the distinguished military leaders of the United Nations to whom our national honor was entrusted. Their dignity, patience, and forbearance in the performance of a bleak, unrewarding task deserve the commendation of each and every citizen of the free world community.

No American, on the other hand, can read these records without a profound sense of shame, frustration, and anger. Our gullibility and naïvete—even after a lapse of ten years—leave one breathless with amazement; and recall the poet William Blake's tart characterization of the well-intentioned person who:

"*...observed the Golden Rule*
Till he's become the golden fool..."

To paraphrase General Omar Bradley's oft-quoted remark, the Korean Armistice Agreement was the wrong truce, signed at the wrong time, and for all the wrong reasons.

Whoever embarks upon negotiations anxious for a settlement will usually have little difficulty obtaining one—that is entirely to his opponent's satisfaction. Bargaining of this sort, which proceeds from weakness rather than strength, has preordained results. To communicate, at the very outset, one's earnest desire to reach a settlement is to relinquish any advantage in subsequent negotiations. In dealings with the Communists, such actions are worse than fatuous: they are positively fatal.

Our objective here is not an evaluation of the Korean Armistice Agreement. The terms of the document which was signed at Panmunjom have been treated elsewhere to an exhaustive and detailed critique. Our concern is, more specifically, the relationship between the truce proceedings at Panmunjom and the conduct of affairs at Koje-do, in terms of their reciprocal influences. The evidence seems incontrovertible that the situation which developed at Koje Island was the direct outcome of our unwillingness to use force in the suppression of Red subversion and rebellion, for fear that stern measures might exert a possible adverse effect upon negotiations.

Was this a rational assumption? Had the Communists given any indication whatever that they were responsive to demonstrations by by the United Nations Command of scrupulous regard for fair treatment of Red captives? In several months of negotiations had the Communists shown by any sign or token that they were amenable to compromise on the matter of the POW exchange?

If the answer to any—or all—of these questions is negative, then it follows necessarily that our posture *vis a vis* the Reds on the handling of POW's at Koje and Pusan was faulty—and fixes, once and for all, the responsibility for the bloody series of mutinies in the UN prison camps.

In the first place, it can hardly be denied that the Communists stood to gain much more from a cease-fire than did the forces of the United Nations Command. Said Robert Leckie:

> "Without doubt, the Communists were ready for destruction by mid-June of 1951. In one year of warfare, the North Korean Army had suffered an estimated 600,000 casualties (including 100,000 men who had surrendered) and was virtually destroyed. In only eight months, the Chinese Communists had lost an estimated half million men. The April and May offensives had subjected the Red Army to a frightful pounding and the May assault had clearly revealed its inability to support large bodies of men moving against modern firepower. Communist Korea was a shambles, its railroads ruined, its communications crippled, its industry close to nonexistent. At Wonsan and the adjacent Hungnam-Songjin steel complex, the United States Navy was continuing the siege which had begun on February 16 and which, maintained until war's end, would be the longest in American naval history. All Communist supply now came from the Soviet Union, and Russia had already shown, in the disastrous May offensive, how she could fail to deliver the goods. Moreover it would be some time before the Chinese received the Russian artillery which would give them a fighting chance against United Nations firepower."

General Van Fleet had formulated plans for a knockout blow, based on a combination of amphibious assaults along the east coast and a breakout offensive from the current UN battleline, the whole supported by United Nations air strength. But Van Fleet's blueprint for victory was discarded—said Leckie—chiefly because the notion of complete victory was by then already in disfavor. In mid-June, the MacArthur hearings were coming to a close, and the Administration had at last spelled out its policy of limited war. The Eighth Army's very victories had already renewed hopes of obtaining a satisfactory cease-fire somewhere along the 38th Parallel. A new amphibious attempt, which might bring the Communist Air Force out of Manchuria again, which might bring fresh Chinese Communist armies south of the Yalu River, which might raise the specter of a second Hungnam, ran counter to all these hopes."

Propelled by such preoccupations, we exhibited almost indecent haste in snatching at the merest twig from an olive branch that Soviet Delegate to the United Nations Jakob Malik waved at the end of a typical Communist tirade over the UN radio. Henceforth we found ourselves in the unfortunate position of acting as suitors to a truculent, hostile, and completely uncompromising victor—a reversal of roles for which we have only ourselves to blame. Officers like Air Force Major General Henry Turner, upon whom the burden of responsibility for negotiating under these dismal circumstances was placed, entertained no illusions concerning the relative strength of the opposing forces. And it can only be marveled that their clear insight failed to make them bitter:

"Let's look at the situation as it is today. You are not threatening our rear in any way. You are not preventing us from rehabilitating airfields or building new ones. You are not preventing unlimited rotation and replenishment of our forces. You do not interfere in the internal affairs of our side in any way. Under conditions as they exist today, you do none of these things. You do none of these things because you cannot—you lack the military capability to do them.

"On the other hand, we do hold islands which threaten your rear. We do keep your airfields unusable by constantly attacking them. We do conduct aerial surveillance throughout your rear. We do limit the extent to which you can replenish your forces by our air interdiction program. We do interfere in your so-called 'internal affairs' by disrupting your internal communications systems and by destroying communications centers in your rear. We do these things today because we have the military capability to do them. Until the armistice is signed we will keep on doing them.

"...We propose only that during the armistice you shall not gain a military capability which you do not now possess. We go even further. We agree to apply the same restrictions to ourselves, even though you lack the military capability today to implement these restrictions by force of arms. But you complain that this is unfair—you who are unable to impose any of these military restrictions upon our side by your own strength. You complain that it is unfair to insist on continuing restrictions through armistice terms which we are fully able to impose, and are imposing on you by military means during hostilities.

"In short, you seek to gain, through negotiation, what you could not win through fighting. You seek to avoid, through negotiation, what you could not avoid through fighting."

None of which, though true, made the slightest impression upon Nam Il and the rest of the Red delegates at Panmunjom.

Apart from the obvious military advantages they sought from a cease-fire, the Communists were clearly bent on extracting every last bit of propaganda value from the Panmunjom proceedings. Here the United Nations Command was at a marked disadvantage. Our military delegates—men of outstanding attainments in other respects—could not match the Communist representatives in political sophistication and specialization in psychological warfare and propaganda. Nam Il was a teacher of Marxist theory and for 5 years prior to the Korean war had held a succession of Communist government posts in education. His Communist Chinese colleague, General Hsieh Fang, was former Chief of Propaganda for the Political Department in Manchuria.

Nothing was too insignificant to escape the notice of these Red officers if it was capable of utilization for propaganda purposes. Vatcher, for example, tells a revealing anecdote about our initial contact with the Communists at Kaesong:

> "It had been agreed in the preparatory meetings that the United Nations delegation and staff would carry the white flag on their vehicles as a symbol of their mission. As the UNC staff approached Kaesong by car, their white flags were clearly visible. The Communist photographers made capital of this event by explaining in their propaganda that the UNC was coming to Kaesong to surrender."

A short time later, in that first session, the Communists pulled another stunt—one that is reminiscent of an extremely funny scene in the Chaplin film *The Great Dictator:* "As Nam Il sat down, Admiral Joy observed suddenly that he was seated in a chair which was considerably closer to the floor than was that of his adversary. Nam Il appeared as though he were looking down on Joy. The latter immediately demanded rectification of this inequality."

The Communists also showed a much shrewder understanding of the uses of the press with regard to the Koje disturbances. Said Vatcher:

> "By the time the United Nations Command presented its 'package proposal' on 28 April the Communists' propaganda sources were running thin. This was well illustrated by the accusation that, at one point, the UNC was training a battalion of monkeys to throw grenades on the front lines. Inasmuch as one of their primary goals at the peace talks was a bountiful propaganda harvest, and inasmuch as the harvest was diminishing, it is not inconceivable that, had the riots not been permitted to occur, or had they not been publicized by the UNC, the Communists might have been amen-

able to terminating the discussions sooner. The Clark report quotes a Communist document which declares that the disclosures of the riots by the UNC was a great victory. The riots and their publicity provided much grist for the propaganda mills of the UNC's opponents...

"To capitalize on the riots the Communists employed every medium. They were assisted by the UNC disclosures of the riots and by subsequent publicity in Western communications media. To illustrate, on 14 May, during the Colson and Dodd debacle, the *Stars and Stripes* newspaper, read by all UNC military personnel in Japan and Korea, carried a two-page spread of pictures showing the good life in a POW camp in North Korea. The photographs had been supplied to the correspondents by the Communists. They were obviously all staged. The previous day the paper carried pictures of the riots in the UNC camp on Koje Island. These depicted deaths, rioting, and massive propaganda signs erected in the compounds by the POW's. The contrasts of treatment were conspicuous."

Vatcher's comments are supported by those of General Mark Clark, who found much to criticize in the UNC and the Eighth Army policies toward press coverage:

"I was aware that there was a suppressed background of violence and bloodshed on Koje and asked permission of the Department of the Army to release a full narrative of past incidents. It was never granted, possibly because of the adverse effect it was believed that this might have on the truce talks. But the skeletons tumbled out of the closet anyway. Members of the press had been barred from Koje during Dodd's capture, but were allowed on the island immediately thereafter. They soon uncovered an eight-month history of anti-UN riots and 'civil war' between Communist and anti-Communist factions that had cost the lives of hundreds of prisoners, four South

Korean guards and one American. Much of this information had never been made public.

"Soon after assuming command, I gave instructions that all events at prisoner-of-war camps be announced officially and promptly. It had been my experience in Italy during World War II that news of incidents, good and bad, should be released to members of the press, in confidence if security required it. This is a practical, not an idealistic approach; someone is going to get the story anyway, and a story always looks worse if it is broken despite official efforts to keep it under cover.

The sensitivity of the Communists to unfavorable publicity had been noted by UNC staff members. According to Vatcher, "Had the United Nations Command beaten the Communists to the draw every time a riot was staged in one of the UNC prisoner-of-war stockades by accusing them before they had a chance to launch an hysterical charge against the UNC, the Communists would have been less willing to continue staging riots." Clark seconded the motion:

"I am convinced that if newspapers had begun to carry stories of the trouble at Koje when it started, eight months before Dodd was captured, the unbelievable conditions which made possible the Dodd incident would have been cleaned up before they really became critical. But great care was taken to make sure the newspapers did not get the story. With the feeling running high that a truce was imminent, the PW problem had been soft-pedaled in the hope that a quick armistice would resolve everything and the fear that revelation of the fights, murders and disturbances at Koje would give the Communists another excuse to delay the truce."

Another point which has nowhere been given sufficient emphasis is the hypersensitivity shown throughout the Korean conflict to public opinion in member nations represented in the UNC. This obsessive concern for adverse publicity in the foreign press reflected—in the present writer's view—a singular lack of perspective and sense of proportion on the part of American political leaders. Without minimizing the importance of moral support, and with due consideration for non-material factors, it needs to be said that the grievous burdens of the Korean war were borne almost entirely by the United States and the Republic of Korea. Excepting the United Kingdom participation, in the form of the Commonwealth Division and supporting air and naval units, contributions to UN troop strength from other nations scarcely added up to a corporal's guard.

Which did not, however, prevent the governments of such nations from seeking to impose restrictions of an insupportable nature on UNC policies and decisions. An example might be offered in the case of the clamor raised by the Canadians when their troops were called upon to furnish assistance to the POW command following the Koje disturbances. Their aversion to having Canadian troops used for guards was immediately deferred to by the UNC, despite the fact that ROK Army and U. S. Army troops were not consulted on their preferences for this sort of assignment.

There was the additional embarrassment of the prisoners of war from 16 nations and the Republic of Korea in Communist hands. Nothing which might prevent the return of an absolute maximum number of these men, if and when a cease-fire could be negotiated, could be hazarded by the United Nations Command. The task of the negotiators at Panmunjom was made even more arduous by the necessity of fulfilling this objective.

To come back once more to the matter of the Koje riots, there can be no question that these disturbances—and particularly the Dodd kidnapping—constituted a tactical victory for the Communists. They scored valuable points in their propaganda campaign against the free world through their calculated program of subversion within the UN prison camps. And their victory is all the more unpalatable in terms of our numerous shortcomings which, to a deplorable extent, made the whole thing possible.

Nevertheless, it is unnecessary to indulge in face-saving rationalizations to recognize that the abduction of General Dodd, which climaxed eight months of Communist instigated violence, was a *strategic blunder* of the first magnitude. The seizure of the camp commander overstepped the limits of UNC tolerance and forced our military and political authorities to take more drastic action than they had contemplated. One could go even further and assert that the kidnapping of Dodd was a blessing in what appeared at the time as a very effective disguise. For it alerted our attention to this hitherto unexplored area of psychological warfare in a way that even the succession of bloody and dramatic outbursts of rebellion had failed to do until that culminating episode. We have since been compelled to study the Koje situation with an eye to the future.

Some of these lessons have already been brought out.

The worldwide struggle against Communist aggression continues unabated. As repugnant as the prospect appears, we may soon find ourselves engaged in another Korea-type conflict. If and when we do, there is every reason to expect a recurrence of some of the circumstances which helped bring about the mutinies of prisoners of war at Koje Island. We must, therefore, be prepared to profit from our earlier mistakes if we hope to prevent another tragedy like Koje-do.

We must select for POW camp commanders only officers of the highest quality and with experience in handling large numbers of men in confinement.

The prison compounds must be kept within manageable size.

Constant surveillance must be maintained, with daily inspections if necessary and a thorough search of the premises occupied by the prisoners. Camp personnel must retain access at all times to every part of the compound.

Enforcement of discipline—it must be conveyed to the enemy—should be placed on a *quid pro quo* basis, in order to afford protection to our own men who might be held captive by the Reds.

"Soft" policies, such as those which permitted Communist prisoners at Koje to fly Red flags and insulting banners, must be replaced by the determination to take immediate action of the sternest nature required to suppress disobedience and insurrectionary tendencies among the inmates.

There must be no negotiation with prisoners, apart from the provisions made for official communication and arbitration under the Geneva Convention. Especially there must be no negotiation *within* the compounds.

The camp authorities must closely supervise the election of compound spokesmen and leaders to insure the fairness of selection procedures, and to forestall any attempts at organized intimidation and subversion.

In addition, there are conclusions of a broader import which emerge from the events that occurred at Koje Island. No amount of Communist propaganda can efface the spectacular victory of freedom over totalitarian serfdom registered in the wide-scale repudiation of repatriation among the Korean and Chinese POW's. "Until the end of the fighting," stated an editorial in *Christian Century*, "the number of those who chose surrender showed that the Communists could not trust their soldiers. This fact will have to be taken into account by the Communists before they renew their aggression... If, beginning in Korea, the tide which has been sweeping across Asia starts to recede, it is highly probable that future historians will locate this decisive conflict on no battlefield, but in the victory which was won behind the barbed wire..."

In an address given on January 23, 1954—Freedom Day—General John E. Hull, successor to Mark Clark as Commander in Chief of the United Nations command, reaffirmed the principle of non-forcible repatriation which both Clark and Ridgway had steadfastly defended. General Hull welcomed the anti-Communist POW's to the free world:

"The 22,000 men who have today regained civilian status and freedom have triumphed in the final battle of the Korean conflict. They fought on for six long months after an armistice was signed, six months which encompassed a move back to their old battlefield, relinquishment of friendly United Nations protection, a cold Korean winter, Communist explanations and broadcasts, and blandishments of Communist agents who had surrendered to penetrate their ranks. They stand as living symbols, providing hope of freedom to the millions who still suffer under Communist oppression.

"This day begins a new epoch in the determined effort of the Free World to resist Communist encroachment on the lives and lands of free people. Today the principle of non-forcible repatriation for which the United Nations has fought so long has been firmly established. From this day on, all soldiers of every Communist army may know of a certainty that they may seek and find sanctuary in the Free World.

"That nearly half of the Korean and three-fourths of the Chinese prisoners of war in the Korean conflict declared that they would forcibly resist repatriation is highly significant. When they made their choice, the practical alternative of freedom in the Republic of China and the Republic of Korea, which now rewards them for their valiant stand against Communism, had not been established.

Yet their hatred of Communism, having experienced it, was so great that even with no certain alternative they forswore their homes.

"To these men who so courageously have resisted both Communist blandishments and Communist threats, the Free World offers not only asylum, but welcome. Their example may well be a beacon to guide others now suffering under Communist tyranny to the sanctuary of freedom and human dignity."

Eighteen months later, in July of 1955, the United States Senate ratified the 1949 Geneva Convention for the protection of war victims. The terms of the Convention had been accepted, by this time, by the governments of 48 nations. Included were all of the Soviet satellites with the exception of Red China and North Korea. Senator Mike Mansfield reported on behalf of the Committee on Foreign Relations:

"During the Korean armistice negotiations the most contested legal issue was whether the parties were obliged to compel prisoners to be repatriated against their will, or whether the detaining power could in its discretion grant asylum to any prisoner who desired it. The United Nations Command maintained that all prisoners who wished to be repatriated were entitled to repatriation, but that international law did not require force to be used if they were unwilling to return. The Communists asserted that forced repatriation was prescribed under the principle of Article 118 of the 1949 Convention on prisoners of war. That article provides in part:

" 'Prisoners of war shall be released and repatriated without delay after the cessation of active hostilities.'

"In the United Nations General Assembly in the fall of 1952, during debates on the Korean armistice negotiations, the Soviet bloc sought to maintain the thesis that the principles of Articles 118 and 7 (which prohibits renunciation of rights by a prisoner) did not encompass a grant of asylum to prisoners of war. The exchanges, in which our own Government took a leading part, developed that the practice of many nations, including the practice of the Soviet Government, was authority for granting asylum to prisoners of war; that the doctrine of asylum was applicable; and that they did not intend to overturn customary law in this respect. Both General Assembly Resolution 610 (VII) and the eventual armistice agreement in Korea permitted the individual prisoners of war a free choice between return and asylum, under safeguards of impartial supervision. The fact that it is an 'unrestricted opportunity of repatriation,' and not an absolute obligation or predetermined fate of repatriation which the prisoner is given under Article 118, was similarly recognized by the General Assembly in Resolution 427 (V) of December 14, 1950, and reaffirmed in Resolution 741 (VIII) of December 7, 1953.

"Members of the Committee, exploring the problem of involuntary repatriation with the executive branch, were informed at the hearing that the United States official position continues to be that maintained in Korea and overwhelmingly supported in the resolution of the General Assembly, and that Article 118 does nothing to change the accepted principles of international law under which asylum is applicable to prisoners of war.

"The Committee unqualifiedly concurs. It finds nothing in the Geneva conventions of 1949 which will compel the United States forcibly to repatriate prisoners of war who fear political persecution, personal injury, or death should they return to their homeland. That article, being intended for the benefit and well being of prisoners, will permit the United States to continue the policy of nonforceable repatriation, while at the same time leaving it free, where necessary, to refuse requests for asylum. The interpretation which has thus far prevailed gives due weight to the word 'release' in Article 118, is faithful to precedent and legislative history, and is fully consistent with the great humanitarian purposes which underlie all four of the conventions."

Thus the principle of non-forcible repatriation has been firmly established as an official United States policy. "United Nations and United States leaders," said Kenneth Hansen, "hailed the application of the principle as a triumph of the ideals of the free world, and the Swiss senior delegate to the NNRC recommended that a conference be convened to rewrite the Geneva Convention to spell out clearly recognition of the principle of voluntary repatriation. But in view of the implications of this principle for the Communist world, agreement on its explicit inclusion in a new Geneva Convention is most unlikely."

To the peoples of the free world, the employment of unscrupulous means to attain righteous ends is morally unacceptable; the rules must take precedence over the winning of the game. Said former Secretary of State Dean Acheson:

> "It is the nature of democracy to recognize that the means we choose shape the ends we achieve. In a democracy, there are no final ends, in the sense of a Utopia.
>
> "The followers of Karl Marx endure the dictatorship of a police state in the delusion that they are ascending to a classless society. But a democratic society cannot employ means which belie and indeed destroy the possibility of achieving its goals. Democratic society, by its conduct from day to day, from week to week, and from year to year, is creating its own future.
>
> "If we continue to move toward our goal of world order in which peace, freedom and justice may be secure, the means we choose to overcome the obstacles in our path must be consonant with our deepest moral sense.

"It is not in the words we profess, but in what we do, and in how we do it, that our ends will be found."

On the basis of past performance, Colonel Hansen observes, "it is apparent that any future conflict between the free and Communist worlds, should the Communists be so rash as to provoke one, will again be fought with the free world making every effort to adhere to humanitarian principles, and the Communists ignoring them."

We cannot look to the future with any reasonable expectations that the special conditions which were present in the Korean conflict will be repeated. Chinese and Korean captives in UN prison camps were able to draw courage, strength, and resolution in their resistance to Communism by having Formosa and South Korea "as spiritual homes about which their hopes and prayers might center." Such a situation, Colonel Hansen warns, might not obtain in a future hostilities involving the free and Communist worlds:

"One of the immense threats of the sprawling Eurasian Communist complex in a global war is that Communism, in an effort to reduce the danger of mass defection of its troops by units as well as individuals, may employ European troops in Southeast Asia, and Asian troops in Europe.

"Parents and armies all over the world have learned by experience that it is wise to send their children to college and their inductees to basic training camps as far away from their homes as possible, to secure increased attention to studies and minimize the temptation to go absent without leave. In the same way, even an anti-Communist Vietnamese might be discouraged from surrendering to the free world in Norway, and an anti-Communist Albanian from surrendering in Vietnam.

"If South Vietnam remains outside the Communist orbit as South Korea has, the Vietnamese would have a spiritual home, a goal to which to direct his hopes. But what of the Albanian, whose only hope could be that the war would result in the liberation of his homeland so that he might return to a free Albania? In addition to China, Korea and Vietnam, only Germany lies astride the Iron Curtain.

"There is a simple solution to this dilemma, one which will at the same time rally a maximum of 'Communist' personnel as individuals and units to the banners of the free world, guarantee them asylum and sanctuary, minimize the mass manpower advantages of the Communist world, and provide for the anti-Communist heroes of the next conflict a spiritual home and goal to which they may direct themselves.

"In any future conflict with Communism, free world national and international policy should declare that only those individuals who are captured in the traditional sense will be considered and classified as prisoners of war. Persons seeking asylum would not be considered as having 'fallen into the power of the enemy,' and they would never acquire the prisoner of war status.

"All individuals, once freed from Communist control, should be screened immediately, to determine their category. To absolve the free world belligerents from charges of 'terrorization' and 'persecution' such as the Communists levelled at the UNC in Korea, a neutral body such as the International Committee of the Red Cross might sit in on or actually conduct such screenings.

"These screenings would produce personnel of two categories: traditional prisoners of war who would choose repatriation to Communist control at the conclusion of the conflict and anti-Communists seeking asylum and sanctuary. The prisoners of war in the traditional sense would be so classified immediately and interned in prisoner of war camps.

"The anti-Communists should be organized immediately in Free Albanian Brigades, Free Bulgarian Divisions, Free Czechoslovakian Corps, until there were eventually Free American, Byelorussian, Esthonian, Georgian, Great Russian, Hungarian, Karelian, Latvian, Lithuanian, Polish, Romanian and Ukrainian Armies on the Free World side...

"If governments-in-exile were recognized by the free world high command, an ideal psychological factor would arise, replacing the stigma of desertion or defection with the patriotic matrix of 'escaping from oppression' and 'joining the forces of liberation.' Existing governments-in-exile could be reinforced by outstanding patriots from the ranks of these escapees, and parallel governments should be organized where they do not already exist.

"Provisional units should be activated among nationals of countries which do not have sufficient personnel at the onset of hostilities to organize battalions and regiments of their own, and from among disabled anti-Communists unfit for further active military service, to guard the prisoners of war, freeing further free world troops for combat duty. *Fully forewarned, such guards would obviate the possibility of Koje-style agitation and riots* [italics mine].

"There would be Communist infiltration, dogged and determined, of course. But the agents who were not discovered in the original screening would have only to open their mouths for the first time in their military units to be revealed for what they were, and delivered to POW compounds. Many of them, just as in Korea, might decide to throw in their lot with the free world rather than to carry out their Communist assignments.

"And the free brigades, divisions and corps would grow apace. 'We believe,' the Chinese anti-Communist heroes in Korea said in their Freedom Day manifesto, 'if there had been troops of the Republic of China at the Korean front at the time of the fighting, defection en masse from the Communist side would have been in regiments and divisions.'

"Army units would not be the only ones to come over. Aircraft and naval crews would seek sanctuary. Communist power would crumble on land, at sea and in the air."

Whether this optimistic situation that Hansen has depicted is a wish-fulfillment fantasy or an augury for the future, only time can relate. Meanwhile, we must strive to preserve our moral integrity against Communist depredations from without, and subversion from within; to resist temptations to meet ruthlessness and suppression with more ruthlessness and suppression; to keep our "bright weapons and shining shield of truth" untarnished in a climate of amorality. To barter our moral convictions for military or political expediency is to abandon that which has been most painfully achieved in the historic struggle of mankind for freedom. "In times like the present," said Abraham Lincoln, "men should utter nothing for which they would not willingly be held responsible through time and eternity... The trial through which we pass will light us down, in honor or dishonor, to the last generation. We shall nobly save or meanly lose the last best hope of earth."

NOTES ON THE TEXT

Preface

[1] A summary of the complex UNC proposal for prisoner exchange, together with a discussion of the legal aspects of the voluntary repatriation issue is presented in the Appendix.
[2] A nautical expression for which landlubbers may substitute *ceiling.*

PROLOGUE: *Operation Honeybucket*

[1] Computed at the old exchange rate. Buying a Korean town today would be slightly more expensive, of course.
[2] If one substitutes "president" for "monarch" in the above passage, it is a remarkably appropriate description of the Korean government prior to the recent revolution which ousted the Rhee administration.

CHAPTER ONE: *At the Inn of the Wooden Door*

[1] See Chapter 5: Brainwashing—U.S. Style.

CHAPTER TWO: *The Face of the Enemy*

[1] "Koreans, more than most peoples of the world, are bound to their soil. A very conservative people of strong traditions, they are born, live, and die in the same village, often never going more than twenty or thirty miles from home. Up on the hill behind the *Ri* are the burial mounds where ancestors are laid to rest, and here on *Hanshik*, or ancestor reverence day—the 105th day after the winter solstice, according to the lunar calendar—every faithful Korean son is expected to go to cleanse the grave and pay respect to his forefathers. This is one reason so few Koreans feel drawn to leave home, and it is another indication of how fearful were the Communist oppressions which made perhaps four million of them flee from the north, before and during the war, to find sanctuary in the south." Robert R. Oliver: *Verdict in Korea*

CHAPTER THREE: *Morning Calm & Rising Storm*

[1] Throughout this book Koreans are identified in accordance with the custom of that country, i.e., family name is stated first, followed by the given name or names.

CHAPTER FOUR: . . .*And Footfalls Lightly Planted*

[2] These irregulars operated behind UN lines where they carried out missions of sabotage and terrorism. Between raids, they holed up in the rugged mountainous region to the northwest of Pusan; and it would have required a full-scale military assault to dislodge them.

CHAPTER FIVE: *Brainwashing—U.S. Style*

[1] Said Rutherford Posts: "No professionally acceptable definition of 'horde' has come out of the Korean experience, although some war correspondents used this arbitrary table of organization: three 'swarms' equal a 'horde,' two 'hordes' make a 'human flood,' and any number of 'human floods' imply a 'bottomless pit of Chinese manpower.' " Soldiers who had once stood in mortal terror of Chinese "hordes" laughed about their earlier apprehensions. A widely circulated joke told of the infantryman who said "I was attacked by two hordes and killed both of them." In a variation, another soldier asked: "How many hordes to a platoon?"

CHAPTER SEVEN: *One-Star Hostage*

[1] In a personal letter to the author, General Colson expressed his extreme reluctance to comment on any aspect of the Koje-do affair.

CHAPTER EIGHT: *Generals Three*

[1] General Clark later remedied this situation by establishing a Communications Zone for 8th Army which relieved Van Fleet of all responsibilities except those pertaining to the direct conduct of military operations.

CHAPTER TEN: *Operation Breakup*

[1] Subsequent to his Koje-do assignment, Major General Boatner served as Provost Marshal General USA, the Army's chief of military police.

APPENDIX I

On January 2, 1952, the United Nations Command formally introduced its plan for voluntary repatriation. Rear Admiral R. E. Libby USN, head of the American sub-delegation negotiating the POW issue, outlined the complex UNC plan as follows:

"1. POW's who elect repatriation shall be exchanged on a one-for-one basis until one side has exchanged all such POW's held by it.

"2. The side which thereafter holds POW's shall repatriate all those POW's who elect to be repatriated in a one-for-one exchange for foreign civilians interned by the other side, and for civilians and other persons of the one side who are at the time of the signing of the armistice in the territory under the control of the other side, and who elect to be repatriated. POW's thus exchanged shall be paroled to the opposing force, such parole to carry with it the condition that the individual shall not again bear arms against the side releasing him.

"3. All POW's not electing repatriation shall be released from POW status and shall be paroled, such parole to carry with it the condition that the individual will not again bear arms in the Korean conflict.

"4. All remaining civilians of either side who are, at the time of the signing of the armistice, in territory under control of the other side, shall be repatriated if they so elect.

"5. In order to insure that the choice regarding repatriation is made without duress, delegates of the ICRC (International Committee of

Red Cross Societies) shall be permitted to interview all POW's at the points of exchange, and all civilians of either side who are at the time of the armistice in territory under control of the other side.

"6. For the purposes of paragraphs 2, 4, and 5, civilians and other persons of either side are defined as those who on 25 June 1950 were bona-fide residents of either the Republic of Korea or the Democratic People's Republic of (North) Korea."

In summary, the UNC proposal provides for the release of all POW's including soldiers of the other side who may have been incorporated into the army of the detaining power. Thus, it is consistent with the first principle advanced by your side that all POW's be released. As regards repatriation, it permits freedom of choice on the part of the individual, thus insuring that there will be no forced repatriation against the will of the individual. It provides repatriation not for POW's alone but for those other victims of War, the displaced civilians. All those who desire it are permitted to return to their former homes. Finally, the proposal provides for a supervisory organ to interview the persons involved to insure that, whatever their choice, such choice will be made freely and without duress."

APPENDIX II

THE NOTED student of international law, Edwin D. Dickinson, gave his views to the *New York Times*, 7 December 1952, in connection with the dispute over the prisoners of war:

"Some of the recent discussions on the question of repatriation of prisoners of war seem to me to be based on certain false notions about international law which should be corrected.

"In the absence of treaty, the competence of states to grant asylum to political refugees is unlimited. Even Andrei Vishinsky in "The Law of the Soviet State" acknowledges the validity of this principle.

"This is no mere moral exhortation. It is a very meaningful and jealously guarded legal power. It is imbedded in the vast network of modern extradition treaties, the written Constitutions of upward of a score of states, and in the domestic law and practice of the rest. The matter is approvingly and succinctly put in Article 14 of the Universal Declaration of Human Rights, adopted by the General Assembly of the United Nations in 1948:

"Everyone has the right to seek and may be granted, in other countries, asylum from persecution.

"States have the power to grant asylum. Everyone has the right to seek it. But there is no generalized obligation to give it—each state must decide on the basis of each request whether or not it will accord it, whether or not under its domestic law it can or should accord it.

"Is it nevertheless to be believed that Article 118 of the Geneva Convention was intended to, and did, deprive parties to a conflict of the power to grant asylum? To deprive the very prisoners the convention sought to protect of the right to seek asylum? To deprive the states involved of the power to propose, or agree to, a plan of repatriation under which some prisoners might opt not to go home? The history of the law relating to prisoners of war and the records of the Geneva Conference of 1947 and 1949 supply the answer to these questions. It is an emphatic "no."

"As early as the Revolutionary War the option of the prisoner of war not to return was respected by the United States under the Treaty of Paris of 1783, when many Hessian soldiers remained in the United States and became valued citizens of the new Republic. More recent precedents are the Treaties of Versailles, Trianon, and St. Germain and the agreements entered into by the Soviets at the close of the First World War with a large number of states. Still more recently there were the Soviet ultimata at Stalingrad and Budapest and the Anglo-French accord regarding hostilities in Syria and Lebanon in 1941.

"An opinion of the Judge Advocate General of the United States Army in 1945 reflected established law and custom in stating that a detaining power was not obliged under international law and the Geneva Convention of 1929 to return a prisoner of war who had strong reason for not wishing to return. The General Assembly itself, in Resolution 427 (v) of December 14, 1950, expressly construed the Geneva Convention and the recognized standards of international conduct as calling not for unconditional return of every prisoner but for an "unrestricted opportunity of repatriation."

"The Conference of Government Experts at Geneva, in 1947, called in order to consider the proposals of the International Committee of the Red Cross for what became the 1949 Convention, was made aware of the fact that some capturing states had refused to repatriate prisoners against their will and that in other cases they had repatriated them anyway. The conference decided to make no provision concerning this problem, preferring to leave room for discretion in formulating agreements or plans of release and repatriation, while assuring the principle that the benefits should be accorded promptly.

"At the Diplomatic Conference in 1949, there was never any question but that a state might permit an individual who, in its opinion, had valid reasons for not wanting to go home, to benefit from asylum. The only point considered was whether it would be wise to require a state to respect a prisoner's wish. This came up in connection with two articles, 109 and 118. In 109 it was decided to require a state to retain seriously sick and wounded prisoners during hostilities if the person did not wish to be repatriated.

"Great Britain and France objected to this requirement on the ground that a state had discretion to retain them anyway, and should be left to itself to exercise this discretion in proper fashion. The winning side, led by Belgium, did not challenge the existence of this discretion, but felt that certain states could not be trusted to exercise it in the appropriate case, and therefore insisted on the requirement.

"Article 118 was adopted the same day the conference had made clear its recognition of the power to grant asylum. An objection to it was offered previously, an Austrian amendment, under which a detaining Power would have been required to respect the prisoner's wish, had been rejected in committee and never reached the floor of the full conference. An objection to it was offered by General Sklyarev of the U.S.S.R. who said he feared that any expression of will might not be entirely free on the part of a prisoner, so that the question of repatriation ought not to turn entirely on his wishes.

"Objections based on immigration law and national policy had been made to similar suggestions in 1947. The most that can be made of this is that it was thought desirable to leave room for the prisoner's state of origin to demand some sort of guarantees that the prisoner's interests would actually be protected. The convention, of course, forbids forcible detention against the prisoner's will and the position of the United Nations Command is precisely to afford unequivocal and impartial guarantees that no force will be exerted to make a prisoner stay or make him return.

"The result reached at Geneva, then, was to preserve the right of a detaining Power to afford asylum, in any case where the prisoner genuinely claimed it; to prevent a detaining Power to respect the wish of a sick or wounded prisoner who did not want to return as long as hostilities continued.

"Finally, from the record at Geneva, at Panmunjom and recently at the General Assembly, as also from what has been said above, it is perfectly clear that the position of the United Nations Command and of the United States is not that a detaining Power at the end of hostilities must admit to its territory all prisoners of war seeking asylum. Neither the position supported by the United States, nor the Geneva Convention, nor the precedent which would be set in Korea would require the United States or any other detaining power in any future conflict to permit prisoners of war to remain indefinitely in its territory."

ACKNOWLEDGMENTS

I should like to thank the editors and publishers of Life, Time, U.S. News and World Report, and Newsweek for granting permission to reprint selections included in this book. I am also indebted to the following authors and publishers for allowing the reproduction of copyrighted material:

BALD EAGLE PRESS

Verdict in Korea by Robert T. Oliver, 1952.

THE CAXTON PRINTERS, LTD.

Tail of the Paper Tiger by O.H.P. King, 1961.

COUNCIL ON FOREIGN RELATIONS, INC.

Korea: A Study of U.S. Policy in the United Nations by Leland M. Goodrich, 1956,

THE JOHN DAY COMPANY

Modern Korea by Andrew J. Grajdanev, 1944.

DOUBLEDAY & COMPANY, INC.

Tokyo and Points East by Keyes Beech, 1954.

Substitute for Victory by John Dille, 1954.

DUELL, SLOAN AND PEARCE

The United States Air Force in Korea, 1950—1953 by Robert F. Futrell.

FARRAR, STRAUS AND CUDAHY

21 Stayed by Virginia Pasley.

FORDHAM UNIVERSITY PRESS

Why War Came in Korea by Robert T. Oliver, 1950.

HARPER & BROTHERS, PUBLISHERS

From the Danube to the Yalu by Mark W. Clark, 1954.

The New Breed by Andrew Geer, 1952.

Soldier: The Memoirs of Matthew B. Ridgway, 1956.

HARVARD UNIVERSITY PRESS

Korea Today by George M. McCune, 1950.

HOUGHTON MIFFLIN COMPANY

Terry's Japanese Empire: A Guidebook for Travelers by T. Philip Terry, 1914.

THE MC BRIDE COMPANY

Decision in Korea by Rutherford M. Poats, 1954.

THE MACMILLAN COMPANY

How Communists Negotiate by Admiral C. Turner Joy, 1955.

FREDERICK A. PRAEGER, INC.

Panmunjom: The Story of the Korean Military Armistice Negotiations, by William H. Vatcher, Jr., 1958.

FLEMING H. REVELL COMPANY

Korea and Her Neighbors by Isabella Bird Bishop, 1897.

Korean Sketches by Rev. James S. Gale, 1898.

THE RONALD PRESS COMPANY

The Koreans and Their Culture by Cornelius Osgood, 1951.

CHARLES SCRIBNER'S SONS

The Captives of Korea by William Lindsay White, 1957.

THE STACKPOLE COMPANY

The Army Almanac, 1959.

U.S. GOVERNMENT PRINTING OFFICE

Hearing before the Committee on Armed Services, United States Senate, Eighty-Second Congress (Second Session): Discussion with Gen. Matthew B. Ridgway re Far Eastern Situation, Koje-do POW Uprising, and NATO Policies, May 21, 1952.

Korea, 1950–1953 by John Miller Jr. *et. al.* Office of the Chief of Military History, Department of the Army.

North Korea: A case study in the techniques of takeover: Department of State Pub. 7118, Far Eastern Series 103 (Released 1961).

Acknowledgments

W.W. NORTON & COMPANY, INC.
In Every War But One by Eugene Kinkead, 1959.
Irma and the Hermit by Irma Tennant Materi, 1949.

Typesetting & Letterpress by the
KOMIYAMA PRINTING COMPANY, TOKYO